Pro-life

a Choice

While Pro-Choices A Life and Right Build Back Good America Today

Ruiz Conner

Table Of Contents

Introduction

"It's my Body, It's my Choice."

bortion is deeply rooted in American history, Every abortion story shared motivates women and pregnant people all around the world to use their sexual and reproductive rights. Everyone, in my opinion, should have access to the reproductive healthcare of their choice. Too many people all across the world have obstacles in obtaining abortions base on different reasons but all traceable to oppression injustice and equality of women and girl in our society

Not all pregnancies are joyful; they may often be frightening and unpleasant. Every year, around 121 million unwanted pregnancies occur, with 73 million of them ending in abortion; nonetheless, we do not talk about abortions sufficiently.

Abortions are common, normal, and acceptable - and there is nothing wrong with having one. Every unvarnished experience shared breaks the silence around abortions and demonstrates that abortions occur for a variety of reasons and generate a variety of emotions, all of which are genuine.

I am delighted to give these perspectives and encourage people to continue talking about abortions in support of others.

The time for silence is passed. If your position on abortion is too complex to fit on a bumper sticker, simply declare Sex labor and reproductive justice.

In the fight for the right to safe and legal abortions in the United States, medical professionals, feminists, and health care activists all agree that criminalizing the procedure does not dissuade women from terminating their pregnancies, but rather makes abortion less safe. The ban of sex work has significant public health and safety implications for surprisingly similar reasons.

Terminating a pregnancy and selling sex are both very personal and usually difficult decisions. People terminate otherwise planned pregnancies due to financial restrictions, unforeseen health issues, and, on rare occasions, coercion by a family member or partner.

Similarly, people engage in commercial sex as a result of choice, circumstance, or coercion. 1

Many of the risks linked with sex work, including abortion, are a direct result of prohibition.

Restore democracy for the benefit of women. Women have a constitutional right to privacy and autonomy in making medical decisions about their bodies. We shall never relinquish that prerogative.

You have the right to believe that terminating a pregnancy is a bad moral decision and that the court erred in its ruling. That is the extent of your rights.

You have no right to impose your morals on me or any other woman. I'm not obligated to follow your ideals or religious beliefs, and neither is any other woman.

Women have a basic right to privacy in our own bodies as well as in medical decisions. No one, including you, has the authority to interfere with a woman's private relationship with her doctor or her medical decisions.

Concerning Roe v. Wade. I don't have a fortune teller. Obviously, you believe so. Nonetheless, I can assure you that women will not tolerate a reversal of our fundamental rights any more than others will tolerate the repeal of the Second Amendment. There is no possibility, under any circumstances, that you will take away our rights, no matter what you do or what the court does. It's as easy as that.

If you're hoping for a Roe v Wade reversal, you may bank all you want, but it won't matter. You cannot force a gay to be straight; you cannot deny them the right to marry; you cannot force a black to attend a segregated school; a Jew to be a Christian; a person to give up the capacity to defend himself; a person to become your slave or property; or many other fundamental rights.

You do not have that option, and you will never have it. No matter how many times you say it or what you say about it, you can't force someone to do what you say.

We did it in the United States in 1865. If you want to fight with women, as it appears you want, you will lose again. It's an impossible struggle to win. You may fight in an unwinnable combat, but you will lose.

For the rest of your life, you may remain outraged, dissatisfied, and even militant about your decisions about women and about losing the battle on women.

If it helps you feel better about yourself, you can embark on a crusade. It will have no effect. Not even a single item.

You will not be able to deprive women of their bodily rights. The story is over. It makes no difference what you want. Your opinions and convictions are irrelevant.

Your war on women is over before it ever began. If you don't believe me, wait till the Supreme Court overturns Roe v Wade.

It won't make a difference. I could write another book on why it won't matter, but I am so sure that your war on women is lost, despite the fact that you continue to wage it, that I don't need to write another book about it; just this letter.

A fact-driven, science-based forum that explains why "pro-choice is pro-life" in every sense of the words. Our Contributors and Moderators are experts in their fields, which include healthcare, law, public policy, and reproductive rights advocacy.

Pro-choice does not imply pro-abortion. Pro-Choice simply means that a woman has sovereignty over her body and the ability to make her own reproductive decisions. Our Pro-Choice forum advocates for abortion rights that are safe, legal, and easily accessible, as well as comprehensive healthcare for women and children. This means that we support Planned Parenthood healthcare services, as well as other organizations that assist new mothers with diapers, formula, safety net programs like WIC, SNAP, and TANF, and Medicaid expansion. We advocate for low-cost or no-cost clinics for both mother and child. We promote sex education, which teaches women how to avoid unwanted pregnancies, as well as accessible and affordable contraception for all women to help them avoid unwanted pregnancies.

Instead of criminalizing abortion, please invest your faith in what our society lacks. Man, for example, should fund the cost of raising the kid to a particular year since he does not endure the hardship of pregnancy because he bears none of the physical weight of pregnancy. His uterus is not in danger of rupture. His blood pressure will not surge over the limit. His kidneys will not fail. His veins are not at risk of clotting. That is how you can tell if American "pro-lifers" are crazy, stupid, or lying. They are opposed to saving newborns. It is not about rescuing babies. It was never about preserving infants. Abortion prohibition does not work.

Nobody has abortions for pleasure. Nobody in history has ever said, "It's Tuesday and I'm bored, so I'll go down to Planned Parenthood for an abortion."

This viewpoint is founded on a form of Christianity (not all interpretations of Christianity) that opposes and burdens the beliefs of others. There is just no legal basis to alter the decision.

If it was determined on an incorrect basis, as some have claimed, the opinion should have been modified to provide appropriate grounds.

In my opinion, the verdict fails on substantive legal grounds, in addition to restricting the exercise of another US Constitutional right, freedom of religion.

I am concerned for the safety of American women who are burdened and may be at great risk of flying to another state to seek an abortion.

Depending on the state, they may be victims of bounty hunters, criminally responsible, unable to travel, or even unable to care for their children or the needs of other family members.

They may face harassment or be forced to prove rape and harassment to others who do not believe them and are anti-abortion.

They may have health conditions that put their lives in jeopardy if they become pregnant. Will they be forced to bear the pregnancy till their lives are jeopardized?

What if they are mentally or emotionally ill and their faith supports abortion? Will women be forced to violate their religious beliefs because the state has decided they must carry a child to term?

Will the lady be forced to have a child and then suffer the agony of placing the child for adoption because she is unable to be a mother for various reasons?

Will our young children who become pregnant by accident or who are sexually assaulted be afraid or unable to seek help, leading them to seek dangerous abortions?

Will abortion drugs also be prohibited? What further invasions of privacy will a woman face? What other invasions of privacy would the government impose on Americans if there is no constitutional right to privacy in the United States?

Will a young adolescent girl commit suicide because the government forced her to carry and deliver an unwanted child? Is that heinous?

How many beautiful daughters, daughters-in-law, nieces, grandchildren, and women will commit suicide, become disabled or die as a result of unsafe abortions, or have a mental breakdown and end up hospitalized or destitute as a result of being forced to have an unwanted child?

How many unwanted children will be born? How many children will be in foster care because the government will not fully fund their needs? How many young people will suffer for the rest of their lives because they lack parents?

Why are women expected to follow the rule that "life begins at conception"? Why is that sort of Christianity the prevalent ideal in a nation where religion and state are officially separated?

Why are women put in a position where it is nearly impossible to have an abortion, yet men can freely distribute their sperm, even in cases of rape, and do not need to undergo a vasectomy?

The government will not force males to undergo medical procedures that violate their bodily rights.

"If guys could get pregnant, Jiffy Lube would have abortions." Betty White Even more vexing is the fact that this choice contradicts the principles of the vast majority of Americans. However, because of the way the Electoral College and the US Senate are structured, it is practically impossible to pass the Women's Reproductive Rights Act, which would legally guarantee the right to abortion.

Instead, the radical right-wing Trump party is considerably more likely to criminalize abortion nationwide just because they can. Mitch McConnell has already vowed that if Congress and the Presidency both turn red again, this restriction would be enacted.

It's ironic that the majority of Republican elected officials and federal employees regard Trump as a traitor who should be imprisoned.

They are well aware that he lied about the electoral fraud.

They know he planned an insurgency on January 6th to persuade Congress to postpone the electoral vote count.

They are aware that he put Vice President Mike Pence's life in danger.

They are aware that he put pressure on and threatened jail time for Georgia and Arizona elected officials and poll workers if the vote was not reversed.

They know he planned a sham voter operation, including in swing states.

They know he coerced the Department of Justice into overturning the election, to the point that DOJ attorneys nearly left in droves.

Nonetheless, these Republicans are willing to lie and violate their oaths of office, as well as the US Constitution, in order to keep abortion illegal, firearms unregulated, and Americans unable to afford healthcare and prescription drugs. In exchange for supporting Trump's Big Election Lie, these same Republicans sought pardons.

Complications from illegal abortion procedures are responsible for 8% of maternal deaths worldwide.

Abortions performed in sterile settings by certified physicians are among the safest medical procedures. Criminalizing abortion makes it more difficult to access appropriate care.

Criminalizing sex work drives the industry underground, where criminals and predators thrive. Because survivors fear punishment, criminalization makes it more difficult to detect and prosecute sex trafficking and other violent crimes linked to sex. The only way to successfully reduce trafficking and brutality against women is to decriminalize prostitution. Several studies have shown a link between the availability of safe and legal indoor prostitution and a decrease in reported rapes, female homicides, and violence against women. Since decriminalizing consensual, adult commercial sex in 2003, New Zealand has seen a remarkable decrease in violence against women and STI transmission.

Body autonomy is critical to both the push to legalize sex work and the feminist campaign for safe and legal abortion access. Individual and collective oppression, marginalization, and sexual stigma — all located at the intersection of race and gender — confuse the binary of individual choice and consent.

No one should be prosecuted for making decisions about their own body.

Chapter One

A Fight For Women Freedom

Overturning Roe v. Wade is merely the first stage in the anti-choice movement's strategy to criminalize abortion totally. We must prepare for a future in which more and more persons will be denied access to abortion therapy. Everyone has the freedom to make the best decision for themselves regarding whether, when, and how to establish or grow a family, free from political meddling. Gender equality cannot be realized without reproductive rights.

Leaders in America did not make abortion illegal until the mid-1800s. Abortion was a natural part of women's lives from colonial times until the first restrictions were imposed. Common law authorized abortion before "quickening," an archaic euphemism for fetal movement that occurs after roughly four months of pregnancy.

Because surgical treatments were uncommon in the late 1700s and early 1800s, medical literature and media commonly referred to herbs and medications as abortion-inducing methods. Reproductive care, including abortion, was unregulated at the time, with certified midwives, nurses, and other unlicensed women's health care practitioners offering it. Midwives were renowned medical specialists who delivered crucial reproductive health care.

Prior to the Civil War, white males were not typically involved in gynecological or obstetric, or OB/GYN, practices. According to Michele Goodwin, a law professor at the University of California-Irvine, half of the women who provided reproductive care were black women, some of whom were slaves; midwives also included Indigenous and white women.

Between 1600 and 1900, abortion was routinely practiced in North America. Many prehistoric cultures were capable of producing abortions... Several states passed anti-abortion legislation throughout the 1860s. The majority of this legislation was imprecise and impractical to enforce. After 1860, stricter anti-abortion statutes were created and aggressively enforced. As a result, many women began to seek out clandestine underground abortions.

When we look at the history of black women in this society, it is apparent how fundamentally abortion laws are built on white supremacy and patriarchal strongholds. The tradition of ignoring black people's humanity is part of America's more than 400-year-old white supremacist system. Although abortion was authorized throughout the country until after the Civil War, the limits for enslaved black women differed from those for white women. Enslaved black women were prized goods. They had little control over their bodies, and slave masters banned them from having abortions. White males held legal possession of black women's bodies. Enslaved women who had access to emmenagogic herbs (plants used to expedite menstruation) had to prepare their own abortion remedies in secret.

The cultural dominance over black women's bodies remained after slavery was abolished in 1865. Today, our white supremacist culture blames black women for having children as well as having abortions, condemning them for practically every decision they make and any form of authority they exert over their bodies.

The present attacks on abortion access are founded on white supremacy.

The Rise of Anti-Abortion Laws in the U.S.

Beginning around the time of the Civil War, a coalition of male doctors launched a crusade to persuade state governments to criminalize abortion completely, with the assistance of the Catholic Church and others who wished to control women's bodies. The male-dominated medical profession wanted to wrest power from the female-dominated midwifery profession, including the right to conduct abortions.

Abortion was illegal in the United States by 1910. Those with money, however, particularly privileged white women, could afford to travel to skirt the restriction and obtain abortions, while others could not.

It has just lately become a heated matter. Abortion was allowed in every state in America throughout the first century.

Legalization and the Fight for Equal Abortion Access in the United States

Abortion legislation was amended in the 1960s. 11 states liberalized their abortion laws in the late 1960s. With its landmark Roe v. Wade decision in 1973, the Supreme Court established the legal right to abortion in the United States.

However, thanks to institutional racism, abortion laws have persisted to target Black and other individuals of color.

The Hyde Amendment, for example, forbids federal Medicaid dollars from being used to subsidize abortions.

Hyde has dramatically damaged Black and Latino reproductive freedom.

Because of the ingrained racism in America's economic practices and policies, Black and Latino communities are less likely to have jobs that provide employer-sponsored health care and are more likely to rely on Medicaid.

Planned Parenthood is striving for universal access to abortion. This struggle is multidimensional. It is about tearing down America's racist structures, such as the economic and health-care systems that force a disproportionate number of Black and Brown people to rely on public insurance that does not cover abortion.

Abortion is firmly ingrained in American history.

Between 1600 and 1900, abortion was routinely practised in North America. Many prehistoric cultures were capable of producing abortions... Several states passed anti-abortion legislation throughout the 1860s. The majority of these legislation were imprecise and impractical to enforce. After 1860, stricter anti-abortion statutes were created and aggressively enforced. As a result, many women began to seek out clandestine underground abortions.

Abortion Laws for Enslaved Black Women

The present attacks on abortion access are founded on white supremacy. Abortion was already illegal in certain US states on Saturday, with legislation implemented mere hours after Roe v Wade was repealed, as cities erupted in protest of the historic decision.

It happened when the United States Supreme Court, more than 50 years after it was created, withdrew the constitutional right to abortion, enabling individual states to decide. It is predicted to result in abortion restrictions in about half of the states.

According to a website affiliated with Planned Parenthood, the US sexual healthcare organization, it is still permitted to go out of state for an abortion.

Utah was one of the first states to prohibit almost all abortions, and its abortion ban went into action the night after the ruling.

Daniel McCay, the Republican state senator who sponsored Utah's "trigger legislation," said it would be dreadful for Utah women to seek abortions in neighboring states, but he had no immediate intention of prohibiting them from doing so.

The "heartbeat bill," which forbids most abortions after the first confirmed foetal heartbeat, also entered into force in Ohio. The 2019 law had been on hold for almost three years until the Supreme Court's verdict on Friday, but hours later, a federal judge agreed to release a federal court injunction that had been delaying it.

When Alabama's state abortion ban went into effect in 2019, it immediately halted abortions, making it a crime to conduct an abortion at any stage of pregnancy, including for rape and incest victims. The lone exemption is for the health of the mother.

Soon after the announcement, Arkansas's health department told the state's two abortion clinics that abortions were now outlawed under a statute that barred all abortions save those conducted to preserve the mother's life in an emergency.

What state laws may be enacted?

On Friday, the lone abortion clinic in West Virginia halted operations. The state has a statute that makes providing abortions illegal, with a three-to-ten-year prison term, but it is unclear how it will be implemented following the Supreme Court judgment.

"Roe has never been enough, but it was the only thing maintaining abortion access in towns like West Virginia," said Katie Quinonez, executive director of the Women's Health Center of West Virginia. People seeking abortions in the state would now have to travel hundreds, if not thousands, of miles, she warned, with underprivileged communities suffering the brunt of the load.

In Missouri, Attorney General Eric Schmitt declared that he would take immediate steps to enforce a state provision that forbids abortion except in "cases of medical necessity." It is the outcome of a 2019 law that contained a trigger provision that would put it into operation if Roe v. Wade was overturned.

Abortion facilities in numerous states, including Arizona and Texas, temporarily suspended delivering abortions while they investigated the legality of continuing.

Meanwhile, other states have committed to retaining the right to abortion. The mayor of Washington, DC, Muriel Bowser, answered by declaring the city "pro-choice," but warning that because it was a district, not a state, it was now susceptible because Congress had power over it.

The Democratic governors of California, Washington, and Oregon have all committed to maintaining abortion rights and aiding women traveling to the west coast for abortions from other states.

Anticipating an inflow of individuals seeking abortions, they declared a "multi-state commitment" in which they vowed to "protect against judicial and local law enforcement participation with out-of-state investigations, inquiries, and arrests" into abortions in their states.

Despite Republican control of the legislature, North Carolina's Democratic governor, Roy Cooper, has promised to retain abortion rights. In reaction to the judgment, he began a fundraising effort on Friday to prevent Republicans from achieving veto-proof majorities in the state in November.

Ral Torrez, the senior public prosecutor and Democratic nominee for attorney general in New Mexico, called on lawmakers to take stronger action to preserve women's access to abortions, especially those from adjacent states.

What do the statistics indicate regarding abortion in the United States?

Over the years, the Pew Research Center has conducted various surveys on abortion, revealing insight into Americans' views on whether the practice should be permitted, among other problems. According to our most recent poll, 61 percent of American adults say abortion should be allowed all or most of the time, while 37 percent feel it should be illegal all or most of the time.

With the United States Supreme Court's ruling in Dobbs v. Jackson Women's Health Organization overturning Roe v. Wade, the 1973 decision that basically legalized abortion nationwide, here is a look at the most recent available abortion data from sources other than public opinion surveys.

What did we do to achieve this?

What is the annual abortion rate in the United States?

It is difficult to find a particular answer. The Centers for Disease Control and Prevention (CDC) and the Guttmacher Institute attempt to measure this, but their methodology differs and their results are contradictory.

The CDC compiles data from the vast majority of states' central health agencies (including separate figures for New York City and the District of Columbia). Its most recent totals exclude data from California, Maryland, and New Hampshire, which did not give data to the CDC. (Read the current CDC study's methodology.)

The Guttmacher Institute collects these statistics by calling every known abortion provider in the country, including clinics, hospitals, and physicians' offices. It uses surveys and statistics from the health department, and it provides estimates for abortion providers who do not respond to its inquiries. The Guttmacher 's totals are higher than the CDC's since it contains data (and, in some cases, estimates) from all 50 states. The institute's most recent comprehensive report, including methodology, may be seen here. While the Guttmacher Institute advocates for abortion rights, its scientific data on abortions in the United States has been widely used by organizations and media outlets across the political spectrum, including by a number of people who disagree with its positions.

The most recent year for which the CDC has published an annual nationwide total of abortions is 2019. According to the ministry, there were 629,898 abortions in the United States that year, a little increase from 619,591 in 2018. Guttmacher's most recent data is from 2020, when it predicts 930,160 abortions nationwide, up from 916,460 in 2019.

It's worth noting that both organizations' data only covers legal induced abortions performed by clinics, hospitals, or physicians' offices, or that employ abortion pills delivered by certified institutions such as clinics or physicians' offices. They do not take into consideration the use of abortion medicines obtained outside of clinical settings.

How has the number of abortions in the United States changed over time?

Since the 1970s, a line graph has depicted the changing number of legal abortions in the United States.

According to both the CDC and Guttmacher, the annual number of abortions in the United States increased for years after Roe v. Wade legalized the procedure in 1973, peaking in the late 1980s and early 1990s. Since then, it has often fallen at a "gradual though constant pace," according to a CDC analysis.

Guttmacher reported almost 1.5 million abortions in the United States in 1991, roughly two-thirds more than the 930,160 predicted for 2020. Looking only at the District of Columbia and the 47 states that contributed data in both years, the CDC recorded slightly more than 1 million abortions in 1991 and 629,898 in 2019. (The long-term trend in the number of legal abortions documented by both organizations is seen in this line graph. The CDC statistics in the figure have been updated to ensure that the same states are tallied from one year to the next, allowing for consistent comparisons through time. Using that method, the CDC estimates 625,346 legal abortions in 2019.

There have been intermittent pauses in this long-term downward trend, most notably in the middle of the first decade of the 2000s and again in the late 2010s. The CDC reported a 1% and 2% increase in abortions in 2018 and 2019, respectively. Guttmacher reported an 8% increase in abortions during a three-year period from 2017 to 2020.

As previously stated, these statistics do not cover abortions with drugs obtained outside of therapeutic settings.

What is the abortion rate for women in the United States? What changes have occurred throughout time?

According to Guttmacher, there will be 14.4 abortions per 1,000 women aged 15 to 44 in the United States in 2020. Its statistics show that the rate of abortions among women in the United States has been steadily declining since 1981, when there were 29.3 abortions per 1,000 women in that age range.

According to the CDC, there were 11.4 abortions per 1,000 women aged 15 to 44 in the United States in 2019. (California, Maryland, New Hampshire, and the District of Columbia are not included in this statistic.) The CDC's figures, like Guttmacher's, show an overall decrease in the abortion rate over time. When the Centers for Disease Control and Prevention reported on all 50 states and Washington, D.C. in 1980, it projected that 25 abortions were performed for every 1,000 women aged 15 to 44.

As a result, both Guttmacher and the CDC report slight rises in abortion rates during the late 2010s. According to Guttmacher, the abortion rate per 1,000 women aged 15 to 44 increased from 13.5 in 2017 to 14.4 in 2020. According to the CDC, it increased from 11.2 in 2017 to 11.4 in 2019. (The CDC figures for those years exclude data from California, Maryland, New Hampshire, and the District of Columbia.)

What are the most prevalent kinds of abortion?

The CDC divides abortions into two types: surgical abortions and pharmaceutical abortions. According to the CDC, 56 percent of legal abortions in clinical settings in 2019 were surgical, while 44 percent were medication abortions using tablets. Since the Food and Drug

Administration first approved abortion pills in 2000, their use as a percentage of abortions has increased over time. According to preliminary statistics from Guttmacher's upcoming report, more than half of all abortions in clinical settings in the United States occurred in 2020 for the first time.

Mifepristone, which lowers hormones that encourage pregnancy, and misoprostol, which causes the uterus to empty, are two pills that are typically used concurrently for medication abortions. Medication-abortion is legal until 10 weeks into a pregnancy.

According to the UCLA School of Medicine website, surgical abortions performed during the first trimester of a pregnancy, suction is commonly used, but the very rare surgical abortions done during the second trimester of a pregnancy employ a method known as dilation and evacuation. How many abortionists are there in the United States, and how has that number changed over time?

According to Guttmacher, there were 1,587 abortion facilities in the United States in 2017. There are 808 clinics, 518 hospitals, and 261 physician offices included.

While clinics account for a minor majority (51 percent) of abortion facilities, they are the sites of the great majority (95 percent) of abortions, with 60 percent occurring at specialist abortion clinics and 35 percent occurring at nonspecialized clinics, according to Guttmacher statistics from 2017. Hospitals accounted for 33% of the facilities that delivered abortions but just 3% of abortions that year, while physicians' offices performed only 1% of abortions.

Simply looking at clinics—that is, the total number of specialist abortion clinics and nonspecialized clinics in the United States—Guttmacher found a 2% increase between 2014 and 2017. There were, however, regional differences. Over those years, the number of abortion facilities in the Northeast increased by 16 percent, whereas it increased by 4 percent in the West. During that time, the number of clinics decreased by 9% in the South and 6% in the Midwest.

Since the 1980s, the total number of abortion providers has decreased significantly. According to Guttmacher, there were 2,908 abortion facilities in the United States in 1982, comprising 789 clinics, 1,405 hospitals, and 714 physician's offices.

Later this year, Guttmacher is expected to release a comparable analysis of abortion providers for 2020. The

CDC does not keep track of the number of abortion clinics.

What percentage of abortions are performed on women who live in different states than the abortion provider?

In 2019, 9.3 percent of all abortions were performed on women whose state of residency was known to be different than the state where the abortion occurred in the District of Columbia, New York City, and the 47 states that provided information to the CDC—nearly the same percentage as the previous year.

Prior to the 1973 Roe v. Wade decision, which prohibited states from prohibiting abortion, the proportion of reported abortions performed on women living outside their state of residence was significantly higher. In 1972, 41 percent of all abortions performed in D.C. or the 20 states that provided this information to the CDC that year were performed on women from states other than their own. In 1973, the same statistic was 21% in D.C. and the 41 states that provided this data, and in 1974, it was 11% in D.C. and the 43 states that provided data.

Expecting that many states would further restrict abortion access, politicians in states with liberal abortion laws, such as New York, California, and Oregon, expect more women from places with less abortion access to travel to their states for abortions.

What characteristics characterize women who had abortions in 2019?

The majority of women who had abortions (57 percent) in the District of Columbia and 47 states that supplied data to the CDC in 2019 were in their 20s, with almost three-in-ten (31 percent) in their 30s. Teenagers aged 13 to 19 made up 9 percent of those who had abortions, while women in their 40s made up 4%.

According to the CDC, which contains data from 41 states and New York City (but not the rest of New York), the vast majority of women who had abortions in 2019 were single (85 percent), with married women accounting for 15 percent (but not the rest of New York).

In the District of Columbia and the 29 states that supplied abortion racial and ethnic statistics to the CDC, 38 percent of all women who had abortions in 2019 were non-Hispanic Black, 33 percent were non-Hispanic White, 21 percent were Hispanic, and 7% were of other races or ethnicities.

The CDC reported from those same 29 states and the District of Columbia that there were 23.8 abortions per

1,000 non-Hispanic black women, 11.7 abortions per 1,000 Hispanic women, 6.6 abortions per 1,000 non-Hispanic white women, and 13 abortions per 1,000 women of other races or ethnicities in that age range.

According to the CDC, 58 percent of U.S. women who had induced abortions in 2019 did so for the first time. It was their second abortion for nearly a quarter (24 percent). It was their third or higher for 11% of women, and it was their fourth or higher for 8%. These CDC figures include data from 43 states as well as New York City (but not the rest of New York) (but not the rest of New York).

A bar chart indicates that in 2019, the majority of abortions in the United States were performed on women who had previously given birth.

According to the CDC, four out of every ten women who had abortions in 2019 had no previous live births at the time of the abortion. A quarter (25%) of women who had abortions in 2019 had one previous live birth, 20% had two previous live births, 9% had three, and 6% had four or more previous live births. These CDC figures include data from 44 states as well as New York City (but not the rest of New York) (but not the rest of New York).

When are the majority of abortions performed?

The vast majority of abortions, almost nine out of 10, occur during the first trimester of a pregnancy. According to the CDC, 93 percent of abortions in 2019 occurred within the first trimester, meaning at or before 13 weeks of gestation. An additional 6% occurred between 14 and 20 weeks of pregnancy, and 1% occurred at 21 weeks or more of gestation. These CDC figures include data from 42 states as well as New York City (but not the rest of New York) (but not the rest of New York).

How often are medical complications of abortion reported?

According to the National Center for Biotechnology Information, which is part of the National Library of Medicine, a component of the National Institutes of Health, around 2% of all abortions in the United States entail some type of issue for the mother. According to the organization, "most complications are considered modest, including pain, bleeding, infection, and post-anesthesia concerns."

The CDC calculates case-fatality rates for women who have legal induced abortions; that is, how many women die from abortion complications for every 100,000 abortions performed in the United States. The rate was lowest from 2013 to 2018, when there were 0.4 deaths per 100,000 legally induced abortions, according to the agency's most current analysis. The CDC's case-fatality rate was highest during the first period studied by the agency (1973–1977), when it was 2.1 deaths per 100,000 legally induced abortions. During the five-year periods, the value ranged between 0.5 (from 1993 to 1997) and 0.8 (from 1978 to 1982). (between 1978 and 1982). Because of the year-to-year unpredictability in the numbers and the relatively low number of women who die through abortion, the CDC calculates death rates over five and six-year periods.

According to the CDC, two women died in the United States in 2018 after induced abortions, both of which were legal. In 2017, the same was true. The CDC reported seven deaths in 2016 from either legal (six) or illegal (one) induced abortions. According to the CDC, the annual number of women killed by induced abortion has ranged from two to twelve.

The yearly number of reported fatalities from induced abortions was higher in the 1980s, ranging from nine to 16, and from 1972 to 1979, ranging from 13 to 54 (the CDC began collecting this data in 1972). (The CDC began collecting this information in 1972.) The reduction in mortality from illegal abortions was one of the causes of the decline. In 1972, the final full year before Roe v. Wade, 35 people died as a result of illegal abortions. The figure fell to 19 in 1973 and then to single digits or nil every year after that. (The number of fatalities from legal abortions has also decreased since then, but with significant variation over time.)

The number of deaths from induced abortions was significantly higher in the 1960s than afterwards. According to data from the then-U.S. Department of Health, Education, and Welfare, a precursor of the Department of Health and Human Services, there were 235 abortion-related deaths in 1965 and 280 in 1963. The Centers for Disease Control and Prevention is a division of the Department of Health and Human Services.

Abortion's racist history and midwifery ban

Sojourner Truth delivered a speech known as "Ain't I a Woman?" in front of a huge crowd at the Women's Convention in Akron, Ohio, in 1851. Slavery was still in full swing at the time, a thriving operation that powered the American economy. Several laws, notably the Fugitive Slave Act, safeguarded that system, resulting in the kidnapping of "free" black children, women, and men, as well as those who had miraculously fled to northern towns like Boston or Philadelphia. Bounty hunters then sold their prey to plantation owners in the South. The legislation denied essential rights to black individuals ensnared in slavery's greedy grasps.

Ms. Truth criticized this heinous organization, which profited not only from unpaid work but also from physical and psychological anguish. Most people remember Ms. Truth's speech for her vivid images of physical labor; black women were compelled to plough, cultivate, herd, and build much like men. Yet much too little emphasis is focused on her denunciation of that system, which rendered black women sexual chattel and subsequently ruthlessly auctioned off black children. This was human trafficking in the American sense, and it had been going on for generations. Ms. Truth begged

"I bore 13 children and saw the majority of them taken into slavery, and when I screamed out in my mother's agony, no one except Jesus heard me! " And am I not a lady?"

Following last week's Supreme Court ruling in June Medical Services v. Russo, it is worth reflecting on the racial foundations of the anti-abortion movement in the United States, which extend back to slavery ideology. Anti-abortion campaigns, like slavery, are based on white supremacy, the exploitation of black women, and the use of women's bodies to serve males. The anti-abortion movement, like slavery, was driven by amassing money and consolidating authority. Anti-abortion campaigns then, as now, had little to do with saving women's lives or protecting children's interests. Today, a person is 14 times more likely to die by carrying a pregnancy to term than by having an abortion, and medical research has proven for decades that abortion is as safe as a penicillin shot—yet abortion is still strictly prohibited in many parts of the country.

Prior to the Civil War, abortion and contraception were legal in the United States and were utilized by both indigenous women and those who migrated to these regions from Europe. Female midwives were the majority of the personnel who offered all types of reproductive health care. Midwifery was multicultural; black women made up half of those who provided reproductive health care. Other midwives were white and Indigenous.

However, in the aftermath of the abolition of slavery, skilled black midwives presented both practical competition for white men seeking to enter the business of childbirth and a threat to how obstetricians regarded themselves. Male gynecologists considered midwifery to be a demeaning kind of obstetrical care. They saw themselves as privileged members of a trained profession with tools like forceps and other technology, as well as the modern convenience of hospitals, which prevented Black and Indigenous women from working in their institutions.

History would later reveal that such technologies were developed on the backs of black women's bodies. Dr. Marion Sims famously spoke of his insomniac-induced "epiphanies," which inspired him to experiment on enslaved Black women, lacerating, suturing, and cutting them while offering neither anaesthesia nor pain treatment. Only recently have the horrors that black women endured as a result of nonconsensual testing by gynecologists in the nineteenth and twentieth centuries been acknowledged.

Successful racist and sexist smear campaigns, meticulously planned for political persuasion and legislative reform, portrayed black midwives as filthy, barbarous, worthless, non-scientific, dangerous, and unprofessional. In a well-referenced 1915 presentation, "Progress Toward Ideal Obstetrics," he stated that:

The midwife is a relic of the past. In civilized countries, the midwife is and has always been erroneous. The midwife has stifled the advancement of the science and art of obstetrics. Her presence both stunts and degrades the first. For many years, she prevented obstetrics from gaining any recognition in the field of medicine... Even when conducted by some of the most competent men in business, midwifery was judged obscene and disgusting.

These attitudes were motivated by deliberate efforts to abolish midwifery and promote white supremacy. As the surge in lynchings, "separate but equal" laws, police violence, and the elimination of vibrant black communities under Jim Crow demonstrated, black

Americans suffered greatly as a result of white supremacy after enslavement, as did Chinese and Japanese workers and their families. Indeed, racist efforts launched by doctors against black midwives resulted in anti-immigrant legislative platforms aimed at Chinese and Japanese workers. Part of this unfortunate history is the Page Act, which prevented Chinese women from entering the United States. This greater anti-Chinese sentiment of the twentieth century became known as the "yellow peril." DeLee and Horatio Storer urged white women to "spread their loins" across the country, sounding the alarm about the threat posed by too many blacks and Asians in the United States.

Gynecologists publicly stated their motivations for combating midwifery: financial gain, recognition, and a monopoly. "There is considerable skill in obstetrics and that it must pay as generously for it as for surgery," Dr. DeLee said in a 1916 study published in the American Journal of Obstetrics & Disease of Women & Children. I will not admit that this is a heinous wish. It is just common decency to reward hard work, self-sacrifice, and competence. " They believed that men should be rewarded, but not women, particularly black women.

To better grasp racial injustice in the anti-abortion movement, recall that American hospitals limited the admittance of African Americans both in terms of practice and as patients. Furthermore, the American Medical Association (AMA) barred women and black people from membership. The American Medical Association, founded in 1847, refused to admit black doctors, reminding them that "you come from organizations and schools that allow women and admit irregular practitioners." As a result, in 1895, black doctors joined the National Medical Association.

The association issued a public apology in 2008 for its strong efforts to destroy Black medical schools, deny Black membership, and engage in other acts that marginalized Black patients and practitioners.

Gynecologists drove women out of reproductive health by convincing state legislatures to eliminate midwifery and limit abortions. Not only did this harm women's reproductive health, but it also pushed competent black women away from medical care. There was no apparent path to the specific skill set DeLee considered necessary for these groups.

Abortion was an effective method for them to describe their desire to give male physicians control over women's bodies. The exclusion of women and black people by the

American Medical Association undoubtedly contributed to this problem.

While many debate whether anti-abortion agendas help black women today, the simple answer is no. In terms of maternal and neonatal mortality, the United States leads the developed world. In terms of maternal safety, the United States ranks around 50th in the globe. Maternal mortality among black women is almost four times that of white women nationally, and 10 to 17 times higher in some states.

Keep in mind, in the context of both Whole Woman's Health and June Medical Services v. Russo, that both Texas and Louisiana, where both cases originated, are regarded as the most dangerous places in the industrialized world for a woman to give birth.

Unfortunately, pregnancy has become a death sentence for many people in the very locations where access to reproductive health care is the most difficult. Many of these states, including Texas, Louisiana, Mississippi, Alabama, and Arkansas, were once slave states. Sojourner Truth's 1851 statement continues to resound as black people in these states fight for fair access to the reproductive care they require. And, as the Supreme Court reinforced this week, The fight for reproductive health care justice and equal access to abortion is far from over. The decision does not advance the equality of impoverished black women; rather, it maintains the other restrictive restraints that are already in place. We have a lot more work to do to ensure that not only DeLee's statements but also his racist and predatory tendencies are gone.

Chapter Two

America's abortion laws' genealogy

It has just recently become a contentious issue. Abortion was legal in every state in America throughout the first century.

A Brief History of Abortion Law in the United States.

Abortion has been practiced since antiquity. Women have had abortions for as long as people have been having sex. The American debate over whether a woman should have the option to terminate her pregnancy is a relatively new phenomenon. Throughout the first century of America, abortion was not even prohibited in a single state.

Abortion is defined differently by different people. When Abortion Was a Crime: Women, Medicine, and Law in the United States, 1867-1973, Leslie Reagan writes in When Abortion Was a Crime: Women, Medicine, and

Law in the United States, 1867-1973. "If an early pregnancy ended, it was said to have 'slipped away' or the menses had been' restored.' "No one thought a human being existed at conception or throughout the first phase of pregnancy before quickening; not even the Catholic Church held this belief." Abortion was permitted until a woman felt the baby move, a condition known as "quickening." Reagan continues, "The public morality concerning abortion and common law were based on the feminine experience of their own bodies at the time."

When states in the United States began to restrict abortion in the nineteenth century, it was often spearheaded by doctors seeking to eliminate traditional healers, or quacks, in their opinion. They received assistance from nativists concerned about women's emerging independence and the country's growing diversity. In 1868, when the West and South were being colonized, anti-abortion campaigner Dr. Horatio R. Storer asked if these borders would be "filled by our own offspring or by those of aliens." This is an issue our women must solve; the fate of the nation lies in their hands. "Who would command those loins, and whose childbearing is desired?" has long been at the center of abortion and contraception legislation.

Abortion was illegal in every state by 1880, save for "therapeutic grounds," which were mostly decided by the medical profession and the court system. In practice, this meant that rich women with better access to doctors were able to get abortions while poor women bled. "The death toll was one clear evidence of the incidence of clandestine abortion," says Rachel Benson Gold of the Guttmacher Institute. "Abortion was acknowledged as the official cause of death for around 2,700 women in 1930—nearly one-fifth (18%) of maternal fatalities recorded that year." Fatalities began to decline with the introduction of drugs to treat sepsis, albeit this was partly dependent on one's condition. "In the early 1960s, abortion accounted for one-fourth of childbirth-related mortality among white women in New York City; in comparison, abortion accounted for one-fifth of childbirth-related mortality among black women." among nonwhite and Puerto Rican women," Benson Gold remembers.

As other countries liberalized their abortion laws, women who could afford it began disseminating brochures on how to make the voyage. Hundreds more ladies visited Mexico, England, Sweden, and even Asia. The California-based Society for Humane Abortion, founded in 1961, detailed how West Coast women may travel as far as Japan to terminate: "If they ask why you need the passport so quickly, tell them you are meeting a tour group in Japan and you didn't realize you could go until just now." Try to negotiate a lower price. Tell them you're a student or a poor working girl with little money. "In the late 1960s, Chicago-based Jane had a renowned hotline where women could call for "Jane" to be routed to an illicit abortion, and members later began performing abortions themselves. By 1973, these ladies had performed around 11,000 abortions. "The women in the service were gutsy, and there was a burgeoning women's movement about taking control of our lives," Jane co-founder Heather Booth said.

Historically, some feminists have felt torn about abortion. Physicians angry at the women with burst uteruses waiting in emergency departments and a budding environmentalist movement concerned about population growth sparked the first push to change abortion legislation. Before Roe v. Wade: Voices That Shaped The Abortion Debate Before the Supreme Court's ruling, Linda Greenhouse and Reva Siegel write, "Feminists sought to free women to participate fully and equally in the workplace, calling for contraception and abortion rights that would give women control over the timing of motherhood at the same time the movement sought public support for child care." "Abortion rights only gradually rose to the forefront of the women's rights agenda, against the backdrop of the 1960s knowledge that sexual expression was a good independent from its procreative purposes." The composition of the United States Supreme Court in 1973, at the time of Roe v. Wade.

The Roe v. Wade decision was decided by the United States Supreme Court in 1973.

Roe v. Wade made no mention of sexual expression or women's liberty. Harry Blackmun, a Nixon appointee, wrote primarily about doctors' rights, ignoring arguments about women's equality but concluding that "the right of personal privacy includes the abortion decision, but that this right is not unqualified and must be considered in regulation against important state interests." The result was dramatic: on a single day in 1973, all 19th-century restrictions were repealed, and states could only ban abortion at the point of fetal viability.

Despite the fact that history has buried it, Blackmun did not go out on a political limb. Republicans nominated five of the seven justices in the Roe v. Wade majority. Even as late as 1972, a Gallup poll found that the majority of Americans (64 percent) believed that "the decision to have an abortion should be totally chosen by a lady and her doctor." Republicans, with 68 percent support, were the most vocal proponents of abortion rights.

Even the most casual news consumer recognizes that this is no longer the case since abortion has become hopelessly politicized. Abortion is not nearly as divisive among most people, let alone politicians, as headlines may suggest. By the age of 45, one in every four women will have had an abortion; until recently, the rate was closer to one in every three.

According to the most recent Gallup poll, exactly half of Americans feel abortion should be "legal only under certain conditions," while a third believe it should be permitted under all circumstances. If you're keeping count, it implies that just 18% of people want abortion totally forbidden. Despite this, the president (who promised during the campaign to select justices who would overturn Roe v. Wade and has already chosen one potential Roe critic) and majorities in Congress and statehouses favor it. Indeed, "there have been 1,187 prohibitions adopted at the state level since Roe v. Wade," according to Guttmacher analyst Elizabeth Nash.

Not only do anti-abortion activists want abortion to be illegal at any stage of pregnancy, but they also want to classify common forms of birth control, such as the intrauterine device, or IUD, and emergency contraception, as abortion. This viewpoint has quickly entered the mainstream. In 2012, a Republican presidential candidate stated, "Contraception, it's working absolutely splendidly." Keep it alone. " Teresa Manning, a contraceptive opponent, now leads the government's family planning program. Manning has stated that "family planning is what happens between a husband and a woman and God," and has long been opposed to the use of contraception. America has come a long way since "quickening."

The argument: you should have left by now.

As the largest giver of global health aid to low-and middle-income countries, the United States should work to eradicate, not exacerbate, health inequities. Yesterday, Representative Jan Schakowsky (D-IL) introduced the Abortion is Health Care Everywhere Act, which would repeal the Helms amendment, which prohibits the use of US foreign aid to fund abortion services in US government-sponsored global health programs. For more than 50 years, we have allowed this policy to exacerbate the problem of unsafe abortion by making essential health care unavailable to many women and girls.

The law itself is plain and unambiguous. It overturns the Helms-Burton Act and replaces it with proactive wording that suggests US assistance "may be utilized to provide comprehensive reproductive health care services, including abortion services, training, and counseling.", and equipment." Furthermore, it lays forth a policy statement for the United States government that recognizes safe abortion as a critical component of comprehensive maternal and reproductive health care that should be widely available and integrated with other types of health care. Furthermore, it contends that the United States should take action to eliminate unsafe abortions and promote safe abortion care by providing funding to and collaborating with impacted governments and service providers.

The Abortion is Health Care Everywhere Act aligns international lobbying efforts on government funding for abortion with those of the domestic reproductive health industry. Campaigners in the United States have worked relentlessly to repeal the Hyde amendment, the domestic version of the Helms amendment in appropriations, which prohibits abortion financing for people who get treatment or insurance from the federal government. The campaign to repeal Hyde has gained enormous traction, culminating in the approval of the Equal Access to Abortion Coverage in Health Insurance (EACH Woman) Act in 2015. The EACH Woman Act now has over 180 House co-sponsors (H.R.1692) and 24 Senate co-sponsors (S.758). The work of the domestic reproductive health community has been critical in undermining the Helms and Hyde amendments' purported political concerns about the use of federal funds for abortion care.

The Helms amendment was introduced in response to domestic abortion controversies. While proponents of abortion rights welcomed the Supreme Court's ruling in Roe v. Wade in 1973, opponents launched a never-ending battle to restrict access to abortion. Their efforts were focused on limiting American women's legal right to reproductive choice, but they also spilled over into international policy. In less than a year after Roe, newly elected Senator Jesse Helms (R-NC) won a victory for the anti-choice movement by successfully presenting an amendment to the Foreign Assistance Act of 1961 prohibiting the use of US foreign aid funds to provide abortion "as a strategy of family planning."

The US Agency for International Development and others expressed misgivings about the plan at the time, citing "potentially imperialistic and hypocritical implications." However, the policy was quickly established, reaffirmed in the annual Department of State-Foreign Operations funding bill, and became simply one of countless boilerplate restrictions on abortion and reproductive health care. By the time Sen. Helms left office in 2003, leaders from both parties had implicitly agreed that neither domestic nor international public funds could be used to promote abortion. In fact, when arguing for the elimination of harmful restrictions like the Global Gag Rule (GGR) or increased funding for family planning programs, pro-choice legislators frequently invoke the prohibition on federal funding for abortion to allay the fears of conservative colleagues concerned that such efforts would somehow open the floodgates for abortion. It is time for pro-choice lawmakers to focus on health equality and remove legislative barriers to health care fairness in the United States. This will be far more successful than appealing to their Republican colleagues, of whom just two in the Senate can be considered strong supporters of family planning and reproductive health care.

The Helms amendment is one of the few surviving federal statutes or rules banning abortion financing that exclude exemptions. Although the Helms amendment expressly says that U.S. money cannot be used to provide abortion "as a tool of family planning," it has been construed and enforced—by Republican and Democratic administrations alike—as a near-total restriction on subsidizing abortion. No exceptions are currently offered for a pregnancy that is a consequence of rape or incest, or endangers a woman's life, but abortion in these circumstances is not deemed a "family planning approach" These exclusions have otherwise had bipartisan support, as most politicians have chosen to avoid the minefield of abortion availability for persons suffering from rape pregnancies. Since Reagan, Republican administrations have defined abortions "as a tool of family planning" as those performed "with the goal of spacing births." It's worth noting that throughout the different incarnations of the GGR imposed by Presidents Reagan, George H.W. Bush, George W. Bush, and Trump, the standard rules implementing the GGR specifically say that the limitation "does not cover abortions conducted if the life of the mother would be threatened if the fetus were brought to term or abortions performed following rape or incest."

Previously, PAI and other activists asked the Obama administration to reevaluate its interpretation of the Helms amendment and make suggestions for changing its implementation. This should have been a straightforward step — and one the president could have undertaken unilaterally — but the Obama administration was unwilling to follow the required procedures. The election of President Trump all but assured that a common sense, administrative correction was out of reach for the foreseeable future.

In 2019, the U.S. The electorate handed the House of Representatives its first pro-choice majority. It was against this backdrop that arguments on Capitol Hill began to take form around the necessity of repealing the Helms amendment. Encouraged by the domestic attempts to abolish Hyde and bolstered by new data that indicates American voters now favor altering federal policy to allow U.S. help for safe abortion care overseas, PAI and other supporters launched in-depth conversations with key Congressional backers. There was consensus that, given these tendencies, it was the best opportunity to fight the Helms amendment and embark on a road toward its repeal.

Repealing the Helms amendment will require a long-term, multipronged, multistep effort. While continuing to build up a solid basis of support in the House, proponents will need to focus attention on the Senate, where a companion bill must be presented, likely during the next Congress. Since the clause appears as both a permanent statute and in appropriations, Helms must also be eliminated from future State-Foreign Operations Appropriations bills.

If the Abortion is Health Care Everywhere Act is voted into law, the good impact on sexual and reproductive health and rights cannot be underestimated. For millions of individuals around the world, it is essentially an issue of life or death. It is estimated that every year, 35 million women endure an unsafe abortion—a main cause of worldwide maternal mortality and morbidity. The large majority of these risky surgeries take place in low-and middle-income countries, where there are considerable hurdles to getting abortion treatment. U.S. foreign policy, like the Helms amendment, should not be an added burden and should certainly not hinder country-led efforts to decrease maternal mortality and promote reproductive rights by liberalizing national or local abortion laws.

Abortion divides various American's State

The supreme court's abortion judgment divides America.

Some Republican-led states will outright ban or severely restrict abortion, while others may impose limits later. At least one state, Texas, is waiting until the Supreme Court announces its final ruling in the case, which is distinct from the conclusion published Friday and may take around a month.

In anticipation of the judgment, several states governed by Democrats have made attempts to protect abortion access. The verdict also sets up the likelihood of legal confrontations across the states about whether providers and anybody who helps women obtain abortions may be sued or prosecuted.

Here is an overview of abortion legislation and the anticipated repercussions of the court's verdict in every state.

ALABAMA

Political control: Alabama has a Republican-controlled legislature and a Republican governor who aim to ban or restrict access to abortions.

Background: In 2019, Alabama lawmakers established what was then the most draconian abortion ban in the US, making it a misdemeanor to conduct an abortion at any stage of pregnancy with no exceptions for pregnancies arising from rape or incest. The only exception would be where the woman's health was at substantial risk. A federal judge ordered an injunction, following the precedent of Roe v. Wade, forbidding the state from enforcing the legislation. In 2018, Alabama voters amended the state constitution to reflect that the state supports the "rights of unborn children" but "does not safeguard the right to abortion." or force the funding of abortion." A 1951 statute made it a crime, punishable by up to 12 months in jail, to induce an abortion, unless it was done to safeguard the life or health of the mother.

The effect of the Supreme Court ruling: Abortions became virtually totally illegal in Alabama on Friday. A 2019 state abortion ban took effect, making it a felony to conduct an abortion at any stage of pregnancy, with no exceptions for pregnancies caused by rape or incest. All three clinics discontinued offering abortions Friday morning for fear of prosecution under the 1951 state legislation. U.S. District Judge Myron Thompson hours later accepted Alabama's petition to lift an injunction and allow the state to execute the 2019 abortion ban. Alabama Attorney General Steve Marshall said it is now a felony to provide an abortion in Alabama beyond the one exemption allowed in the 2019 law, which is for the purpose of the mother's health. Doctors who break the act can face up to 99 years in prison. Marshall said the state will also aim to overturn previous injunctions that blocked prior abortion restrictions, including a requirement for doctors who perform abortions to have hospital admitting privileges.

Some Republican lawmakers have stated they would prefer to see the state replace the 2019 ban with a less draconian bill that would allow exceptions in circumstances of rape or incest. Proponents suggested the 2019 restriction was purposely stringent in the hope of sparking a legal challenge to Roe.

ALASKA

Political control: Republicans now enjoy a majority of seats in the state Legislature, but the House is managed by a bipartisan coalition consisting primarily of Democrats. This year, 59 of the 60 legislative seats are up for election. Gov. Mike Dunleavy is running for reelection as a Republican who believes life begins at conception.

The Alaska Supreme Court has read the right to privacy in the state constitution as including abortion rights.

Given the state's previous history, the decision of the United States Supreme Court is not likely to have an immediate impact on abortion rights in Alaska.

Voters in the autumn will be asked if they want to summon a constitutional convention, an issue that comes up every 10 years. Many conservatives who want to overhaul how judges are selected and do away with the concept that the constitution's right to privacy clause allows for abortion rights see an opportunity in calling for a convention. Recent efforts to force a constitutional change through the Legislature have been futile.

ARIZONA,

Both legislative houses are controlled by Republicans, who often adopt abortion restrictions that for the past eight sessions have been promptly signed by Republican Gov. Doug Ducey, an abortion opponent.

Background: Arizona law allows abortion through about 22 weeks, but the Legislature adopted a 15-week abortion limit in March, mirroring the Mississippi legislation that was litigated before the U.S. Supreme Court. It will take effect 90 days after the Legislature adjourns, which it did on Saturday. Current constraints include bans on abortions because of gender and a 2021 law that makes it a crime for a doctor to terminate a pregnancy because the youngster has a survivable genetic condition. Arizona also has pre-statehood legislation remaining on the books that would outlaw all abortions, but it has not been implemented since Roe was ruled.

Ducey has claimed in media interviews that the bill he signed in late March takes precedence over the entire prohibition that remains on the books. But the statute he signed expressly specifies it does not invalidate the entire abortion prohibition in force for more than 100 years. Ducey's tenure is over in January, and he will depart office. Abortion providers across the state suspended all services after the court ruled Friday because of fears that the pre-Roe prohibition may leave physicians, nurses, and other professionals in danger of prosecution.

Abortion-rights proponents in Arizona have begun a long-shot quest to embed the right to abortion in the state constitution. Rolling out weeks after the draft U.S. Supreme Court opinion showing Roe would be overturned was leaked, proponents must gather more than 356,000 signatures by July 7 to get the initiative on the November ballot. Voters would then be free to decide.

Arkansas,

Arkansas' legislature is dominated by Republicans who have endorsed hundreds of abortion bans and restrictions in recent years. Republican Gov. Asa Hutchinson likewise has favored limits on abortion with limited exceptions. He's term-limited and leaves office in January. Republican nominee Sarah Sanders, press secretary to departing President Donald Trump, is widely favored in the November election to succeed him.

Arkansas previously had a regulation barring most abortions 20 weeks into a woman's pregnancy, with exceptions for rape, incest, and the life of the mother. The state has multiple other laws that have been thrown down or blocked by judges in recent years, including an explicit abortion ban adopted last year that doesn't contain rape or incest exceptions. That ban has been suspended by a federal judge, and the state has appealed.

Effect of Supreme Court ruling: Arkansas has a statute approved in 2019 that bans practically all abortions now that Roe is overruled. That rule, along with the outright ban that's been halted by a federal court, only allows exceptions to safeguard the life of the mother in a medical emergency. Hutchinson has stated he thinks prohibitions should contain rape and incest exclusions, but he has not called on the Legislature to add them to any of the bans.

Hours after Friday's verdict, Attorney General Leslie Rutledge signed a certification that Roe had been overridden. That certification enables the state's "trigger ban" to take effect immediately. The single exemption under that regulation is to preserve the life of the mother in a medical emergency. The Legislature isn't due to meet until January, but Hutchinson is considering convening a special session to take up tax relief measures. The Republican governor said Friday he does not plan on asking lawmakers to investigate adding rape and incest exceptions to the state's prohibition.

CALIFORNIA

Political power: Democrats who advocate access to abortion control all statewide political seats and have a large majority in the state Legislature.

Background: California prohibited abortion in 1850, except where the life of the mother was in jeopardy. The legislation was modified in 1967 to permit abortions in the instances of rape, incest, or if a woman's mental health was at risk. In 1969, the California Supreme Court deemed the state's original abortion statute to be unconstitutional but kept the 1967 law in place. In 1972, California voters added a "right to privacy" to the state constitution. Since then, the state Supreme Court has construed that "right to privacy" as a right to access abortion, enabling minors to receive an abortion without their parents' approval and use public financing for abortions in the state's Medicaid program. California now mandates private health insurance plans to cover abortions and does not allow them to charge items such as as co-pays or deductibles for the operation.

The effect of the Supreme Court ruling: Abortion will remain lawful in California prior to the viability of a fetus. Democratic Gov. Gavin Newsom has vowed to make California a sanctuary for women who reside in other states where abortion is illegal or severely limited. The number of women who travel to the state for abortions is likely to grow dramatically.

What comes next: The state legislature is considering 13 bills that would improve or expand abortion access. The proposals are based on a report by the Future of Abortion Council, which Newsom established last year to study reproductive rights in California. They include proposals to help pay for women from other states to travel to California for abortions; to prohibit the enforcement of out-of-state civil judgments against California abortion providers and volunteers; and to expand the number of people who can provide abortions by allowing some nurse practitioners to perform the procedure without the supervision of a doctor. In addition, lawmakers seek to place a constitutional amendment on the November ballot that would expressly safeguard the right to abortion and contraception.

COLORADO

Political power: The Democrats who control the Colorado legislature, as well as the state's Democratic governor, favor abortion rights.

Background: A state law passed in 1967 legalized abortion up to 16 weeks of pregnancy. Abortion has been legal since then, despite several legislative initiatives and voter campaigns to limit or abolish the procedure. Similar efforts have been repeatedly defeated by Colorado voters, the most recent in 2020, which would have restricted abortion throughout the third trimester of pregnancy. Colorado Gov. Jared Polis signed legislation ensuring the right to abortion in state laws in 2022. The Act guarantees access to reproductive health care before and after pregnancy and prohibits local governments from imposing their own restrictions. It also states that fertilized eggs, embryos, and fetuses lack autonomy. Abortion rights activists are planning a ballot initiative in 2024 to add abortion rights to the state constitution and reverse a 1980s constitutional amendment that prohibits public funding for abortion.

The Supreme Court's decision will have no immediate impact on Colorado law, but providers are ready for an influx of out-of-state patients. Democratic House Majority Leader Daneya Esgar says legislators must consider how to invest in a health-care workforce to ensure Colorado can meet the predicted demand. According to Colorado's health department, there will be 11,580 abortions in the state in 2021, with 14 percent of them being for non-residents. There were nearly 900 non-residents from Texas, Wyoming, and Nebraska.

It's difficult to predict how many additional patients from surrounding states may seek treatment now that Roe v. Wade has been overturned. However, the Texas legislation may encourage more visitors to visit. Oklahoma now has an early pregnancy abortion restriction; Utah and Wyoming have trigger laws prohibiting abortion now that Roe v. Wade has been reversed; and the Kansas Constitution guarantees abortion rights, but Republican lawmakers placed an effort to repeal it on the August primary ballot.

Political power: The Democrats who control the Connecticut General Assembly, as well as the state's Democratic governor, favor abortion rights.

Background: Connecticut passed laws providing women legal access to abortion in 1990. It was praised at the time for being a rare compromise between abortion rights supporters and opponents, having passed with overwhelming bipartisan support. It backed a woman's unequivocal right to an abortion "before viability of the fetus," as well as later-term abortions "essential to protect the pregnant woman's life and health. " It also declared unconstitutional state legislation that made having or conducting abortions unconstitutional prior to Roe v. Wade, and it required that patients under the age of 16 get counseling about their options." Gov. Ned Lamont signed legislation last year to protect medical practitioners and patients from out-of-state legal procedures. The same law allows for aspiration abortions to be performed by advanced practice registered nurses, nurse-midwives, or physician assistants within the first 12 weeks of a pregnancy.

The impact of the Supreme Court's decision: Connecticut Attorney General William Tong, a Democrat, has committed to fighting any attempt to alter the state's abortion rights law. "Let us not mince our words. During a recent news conference, Tong promised abortion rights campaigners, "They will come for us." "We will fight it tooth and nail." Connecticut will be present and fighting in whatever court or location. The government is already involved in high-profile abortion cases around the country. While Connecticut is surrounded by traditionally pro-abortion states, the state is ready for an influx of out-of-state patients seeking abortions now that Roe v. Wade has been overturned.

What comes next: Connecticut's new legislation protecting abortion providers from the bans of other states goes into effect on July 1. It creates a legal cause of action for providers and others who are sued in another state, allowing them to recoup some of their legal expenses. It also limits the governor's discretion to extradite someone suspected of carrying out an abortion, as well as Connecticut courts' and agencies' involvement in that litigation. There has been discussion about amending the state constitution to make abortion more difficult to overturn, but this would be a multi-year process.

DELAWARE

Political power: Democrats control the governor's office and both chambers of the Delaware legislature, and they have made major efforts to ensure abortion access.

Following President Donald Trump's victory, Delaware became the first state to legislate the right to abortion. A law signed by Catholic Gov. John Carney guarantees the unlimited right to an abortion before a fetus is pronounced "viable." The act defines viability as the point in a pregnancy when, in a doctor's "good faith medical opinion," there is a significant likelihood that the fetus will live outside the uterus without the use of extraordinary medical procedures. Abortion after embryonic viability is also permitted if, in a doctor's "good faith medical opinion," abortion is necessary for the preservation of the woman's life or health, or if there is a reasonable likelihood that the fetus cannot live without extraordinary medical efforts. The act eliminated earlier code restrictions on abortions, much of which had previously been declared unenforceable by Delaware's attorney general in 1973 in the aftermath of the Supreme Court's Roe v. Wade and Doe v. Bolton decisions. Carney signed legislation in April of this year allowing physician assistants and advanced practice registered nurses to supply abortion-inducing drugs like mifepristone and misoprostol.

"In Delaware, the privacy protections of Roe v. Wade are written into state law, insuring citizens have access to legal abortion services even if Roe were to be undone at the federal level," Democratic lawmakers stated earlier this month in introducing legislation expanding access to abortions. The bill, which is expected to be passed by the end of June, allows physician assistants, certified nurse practitioners, and nurse midwives to perform abortions prior to viability. It also provides many legal protections for abortion providers and patients, including out-of-state residents who have abortions in Delaware. These provisions include protection against civil litigation in other jurisdictions relating to pregnancy abortion, as well as protection from extradition to other states for criminal offenses related to pregnancy termination.

According to state health officials, 2,042 abortions were performed in Delaware in 2019, with 1,765 performed on Delaware residents and 277 performed on nonresidents. Given that neighboring Maryland and New Jersey already have liberal abortion-access legislation, Delaware is unlikely to see a large influx of women traveling from out of state to get abortions if Roe v. Wade is overturned. In adjacent Pennsylvania, where Republicans control both houses of the legislature, future abortion access may be determined by the outcome of the governor's race this year.

COLUMBIA DISTRICT

Democrats completely rule the city government of the nation's capital, with a Democratic mayor and a D.C. Council divided between Democrats and nominal independent members who are always, always, Democrats.

Background: Abortion is legal in the District of Columbia at all stages of pregnancy, as stated by the Supreme Court in the 1971 decision, United States v. Vuitch. However, the United States Congress has oversight authority over D.C. law, and Congress has previously prohibited the city from using local funds to pay for abortions for Medicaid recipients.

The impact of the Supreme Court decision: Elected officials in Washington, D.C. are concerned that Congress may seek to restrict abortion access, especially if Republicans win control of the House of Representatives in the midterm elections later this year. President Joe Biden might veto such a move, but such protection is contingent on political considerations and is not guaranteed.

Local governments have vowed civil disobedience in the face of any Congressional legislation that would restrict local abortion access. The D.C. Council is considering legislation that would designate Washington, D.C. as a "sanctuary city" for those fleeing countries where abortion is outlawed. According to official data, the majority of women seeking abortions in Washington already come from out of state. These figures might rise if new Republican Gov. Glenn Youngkin moves to restrict abortion access in neighboring Virginia.

FLORIDA

Political power: Republicans control both chambers of the Florida Legislature, and the state's Republican governor put a ban on abortions beyond 15 weeks into law this year.

Background: Abortion was legal in Florida until the 24th week of pregnancy, but politicians have been limiting access in recent years by enforcing a one-day waiting period and notifying the parents of a pregnant minor before an abortion may be performed. In anticipation of the United States Supreme Court's decision to overturn Roe v. Wade, the Legislature enacted a ban on abortions beyond the 15th week, except to save the mother's life, prevent serious injury, or if the fetus has a fatal condition. Exclusions are not permitted in cases where pregnancies were caused by rape or incest. Gov. Ron DeSantis called the Act "the most critical safeguard for life that this state has undertaken in a generation."

The decision of the Supreme Court establishes Florida's 15-week ban on a firm legal foundation, at least under federal law. However, the bill is already being challenged in state court on the grounds that it violates a right to privacy guarantee in the state constitution.

Florida's 15-week limit takes effect on July 1st, but legal challenges are ongoing. Despite the fact that only about 2% of abortions in Florida occur after the 15th week, abortion rights advocates have expressed concern about declining access to the procedure not only for Floridians but also for residents of neighboring Southern states, where restrictions have historically been stricter than in Florida.

GEORGIA,

Georgia has a Republican legislature and governor that support abortion restrictions, but all are up for re-election this November. A Democrat might be elected governor.

Background: In 2019, Georgia lawmakers passed a bill by a single vote that makes most abortions illegal after six weeks of pregnancy, when a fetal heart beat may be detected. The bill differs from past so-called "heartbeat" initiatives in that it includes language designating a fetus as a person for state-law purposes like income tax deductions and child support. The measure was immediately halted by a federal judge, who ruled it was illegal, and the state appealed to the 11th U.S. Circuit Court of Appeals. The 11th Circuit stated it would decide on the appeal after the United States Supreme Court issued its decision in the Mississippi case.

The impact of the Supreme Court's decision is that On the same day that the Supreme Court reversed Roe v. Wade, Georgia's attorney general sought the 11th Circuit to reverse the lower court's decision and enable the state's abortion statute to take effect. The Eleventh Circuit ordered the parties to provide papers within three weeks explaining the impact, if any, of the Supreme Court's decision on the Georgia appeal. If the bill is implemented, it will prohibit the vast majority of abortions now performed in Georgia—around 87 percent, according to providers. The change might occur in the midst of hotly fought races for governor and U.S. Senate in Georgia. Democratic U.S. Sen. Raphael Warnock and governor-elect Stacey Abrams both say they want to protect abortion rights. Republican Senate candidate Herschel Walker and Republican Gov. Brian Kemp both support limitations.

Some Republican legislators and candidates want Georgia to go even further and outlaw abortion completely, but Kemp is unlikely to call a special session before the general election in November. When lawmakers reconvene in January for their annual session, they are expected to contemplate more measures. The Legislature or the courts must decide if the measures designating a fetus as a person are practicable.

HAWAII

Political power: The governor of Hawaii is a Democrat, and Democrats hold more than 90 percent of the seats in the state's House and Senate.

Background: Hawaii became the first state in the US to decriminalize abortion at the request of a woman in 1970. The state permits abortion until a fetus is viable outside of the womb. Following that, it is authorized if a patient's life or health is in danger. For many years, the therapy could only be administered by licensed physicians. The state passed legislation last year that allows advanced practice care nurses to perform in-clinic abortions throughout the first trimester. This helps women on more isolated islands who have been traveling to Honolulu for abortions due to a lack of doctors in their villages. The law allows nurses to use medications to end a pregnancy and perform aspiration abortions, which are small surgeries in which a vacuum is used to empty a woman's uterus.

Existing Hawaii law permits abortions, but Gary Yamashiroya, a spokesperson for the state attorney general's office, has indicated that the attorney general is carefully reviewing steps Hawaii would take to protect and extend reproductive rights if Roe is overturned. "Despite the outcome," he continued, "our state is devoted to reproductive freedom and choice. "There is strong political support for abortion rights. Anti-abortion legislation is rarely debated in the state legislature. They haven't made it out of committee when they have been When the Supreme Court's draft decision overturning Roe became public, Gov. David Ige issued a statement in support of abortion rights. "Despite of what the Supreme Court rules, I will fight to safeguard a woman's right to choose in the state of Hawaii," he stated. Earlier this month, the Hawaii State Commission on the Status of Women reported that 72 percent of state Senate members and 53 percent of state House members signed a pledge in support of abortion rights.

IDAHO

Political power: Republicans control both the House and Senate and, like the state's Republican governor, oppose abortion access.

Following the 1973 Roe v. Wade decision by the United States Supreme Court, Idaho passed legislation allowing abortions in the first and second trimesters up to viability at around 23 to 24 weeks. Abortions after viability are permitted primarily to save the mother's life or in cases of nonviable fetuses. This year, lawmakers passed a Texas-style law prohibiting abortions after six weeks of pregnancy and allowing family members to sue medical practitioners who perform abortions. This bill is on hold while Planned Parenthood files a lawsuit. The Idaho Supreme Court will hear oral arguments in August.

The Supreme Court's decision triggers a 2020 Idaho law prohibiting all abortions except in cases of suspected rape or incest, or to protect the mother's life, which will go into effect in 30 days. According to the law, the person performing the abortion might face criminal prosecution and up to five years in prison. In cases of rape or incest, the law requires pregnant women to file a police report and show a copy of the report to their doctor before having an abortion. If the Idaho Supreme Court upholds the state's Texas-style abortion prohibition and upholds Roe v. Wade, a medical professional who performs an abortion in Idaho may face a lawsuit and criminal sanctions.

Pregnant women who want abortions will have to travel out of state; the closest abortion providers will be in Washington, Oregon, Nevada, and Colorado. Planned Parenthood has leased land in the Idaho-Oregon border town of Ontario and claims it is prepared for an influx of patients seeking abortions. Some Republican lawmakers in Idaho are expected to introduce new legislation criminalizing abortion medicine and emergency contraception.

ILLINOIS

Political control: Illinois is primarily Democratic, with legislation that allows for broader abortion access than most states. Democrats have veto-proof supermajorities in both the House and Senate, and J.B. Pritzker, the Democratic first-term governor running for reelection this year, has urged peaceful public protests to protect the constitutional right to abortion.

Background: In Illinois, abortion is legal and can only be prohibited beyond the time of viability, when a fetus is determined to be capable of survival outside the womb. Medical research suggests viability at 24 to 26 weeks, but the Illinois statute does not specify a schedule, asserting that a medical practitioner can determine viability in each case. Abortions are also legal after viability to protect the patient's life or health.

The Supreme Court's decision will have no effect on abortion availability in Illinois. Following the Roe v. Wade decision in 1973, the Illinois Abortion Act of 1975 legalized abortion but included a "trigger law" that would reinstate the prohibition if Roe was overturned. This trigger clause was repealed in 2017 as part of legislation requiring Medicaid and state employees' group health insurance to cover abortions. The 2019 Reproductive Health Act replaced the 1975 act, significant portions of which were never implemented because they were deemed unconstitutional.

In recent months, Illinois, like other jurisdictions providing abortion access, has seen a constant trickle of patients crossing the state line for abortions, and those numbers are expected to rise. Planned Parenthood of Illinois anticipates an increase of 20,000 to 30,000 patients in the first year following the Roe v. Wade decision.

INDIANA

Political control: Indiana has a Republican-controlled legislature and a Republican governor who supports abortion restrictions.

Background: Abortion is legal in Indiana until roughly 20 weeks, with a few exceptions for medical reasons. Patients must wait 18 hours before having an abortion. Medical personnel must inform patients about the risks of abortion and claim that the fetus can feel pain for about 20 weeks, which is debatable. Providers must report abortion-related complications; failure to do so might result in a misdemeanor, 180 days in jail, and a $1,000 fine. Many restrictions in Indiana have been rejected by federal courts, including an attempt to criminalize a common second-trimester abortion procedure and a regulation requiring doctors to notify pregnant women about a disputed medication that may potentially reverse a drug-induced abortion.

No immediate changes are expected as a result of the Supreme Court decision. However, legislators unwilling to wait until the 2023 session may press Indiana Gov. Eric Holcomb to call a special session this summer to begin changing the state's abortion laws.

Republican legislative leaders indicated Friday that they anticipated lawmakers tightening Indiana's abortion legislation during a special legislative session beginning July 6, but they provided no details on what restrictions would be proposed. Though state law allows legislators to address any matter, Republican Gov. Eric Holcomb called a special session of the Legislature earlier this week to discuss a tax refund proposal.

IOWA

Political control: Republicans dominate Iowa's legislature, which wants to ban or restrict abortion access, and a Republican governor who agrees is up for reelection this year.

Background: Iowa permits most abortions until the 20th week of pregnancy, when they're outlawed except to save a patient's life or avert a substantial and irreversible physical impairment of a vital bodily function. In 2018, the state Supreme Court pronounced access to abortion a "fundamental" right under the state constitution, affording wider safeguards to abortion rights than the U.S. Constitution. The state's highest court, now ruled by a conservative majority, overturned that decision on June 17, enabling state legislation mandating a 24-hour waiting period to take effect immediately. In district court, that mandate is being challenged.

The impact of the Supreme Court decision: Nothing is expected to change in Iowa right now. The Republican-controlled Legislature has sought to place an amendment on the ballot in 2024 declaring that the state constitution does not include a right to abortion; but, with Roe overturned, Iowa legislators may criminalize abortion without completing the lengthy process.

Now that the Iowa Supreme Court has issued its 2018 decision, the state Legislature can convene a special session this summer to enact abortion restrictions. Republicans may still try to have the constitutional amendment on the ballot in 2024.

KANSAS

Political control: Kansas has a Republican-controlled legislature that wants to ban or restrict abortion access but a Democratic governor who favors access and is up for re-election this year.

Background: Most abortions in Kansas are legal until the 22nd week of pregnancy, when they can only be performed to save a patient's life or to avoid "significant and permanent physical impairment of a vital bodily function." In 2019, the state Supreme Court ruled that access to abortion is a "fundamental" right under the state constitution, providing broader protections for abortion rights than the US Constitution does today. However, state law prohibits physicians from providing abortion medicines via telemedicine consultations.

The Supreme Court's decision has no immediate impact on Kansas. The state Supreme Court halted the execution of a 2015 legislative ban on a popular second-trimester procedure, and abortion opponents fear that a slew of additional restrictions may be challenged in the near future. The GOP-controlled Legislature responded by putting the constitutional amendment on the ballot for the Aug. 2 primary, when turnout is projected to be substantially lower than in a general election and a bigger number of Republicans will likely vote. The amendment would declare that abortion is not a right guaranteed by the state constitution. It will give Congress the authority to regulate abortion as far as the federal courts will allow.

If voters approve the amendment, the Legislature must still enact the extra restrictions, and lawmakers are not in session until January 2023. They could call a special session with two-thirds support, but they're more likely to wait until voters decide whether to give Democratic Gov. Laura Kelly a second term in November.

KENTUCKY

Political control: Republicans have a supermajority in the Kentucky Legislature and have been restricting abortion rights since the 2016 election, despite vetoes from Democratic Gov. Andy Beshear, who supports abortion rights and is up for re-election in 2023.

Although Kentucky prohibits abortion beyond 20 weeks, all abortion services were temporarily halted in April when the legislature imposed additional restrictions and reporting requirements on the state's two abortion clinics. Both clinics in Louisville stated they ceased abortions because state officials had not released guidelines on how to comply with the new legislation. Noncompliance may result in large penalties, prison terms, and the loss of medical and facility licenses. Abortions resumed after a federal judge temporarily blocked key portions of the measure, including a provision prohibiting abortions after 15 weeks of pregnancy.

As a result of the Supreme Court's decision, abortion services in Kentucky became illegal immediately, thanks to a "trigger statute" enacted in 2019. The plan includes a narrow exception that allows abortion to prevent the death or substantial harm to a pregnant woman. Kentucky residents will be able to vote in November on a proposed amendment to the state constitution saying that there is no right to abortion.

Abortion activists believe the April suspension of abortion services foreshadowed what would happen in Kentucky and other Republican-leaning states if Roe v. Wade was overturned. It will almost certainly put a stop to other legal challenges to Kentucky abortion laws, including a 2018 provision that abortion-rights activists argue would effectively criminalize a standard abortion method in the second trimester of pregnancy. In March, the United States Supreme Court determined that Kentucky's Republican attorney general, Daniel Cameron, could defend the measure that had been struck down by lower courts.

LOUISIANA

Political control: Republicans dominate Louisiana's legislature, which seeks to outlaw or restrict abortion access. Its Democratic and Catholic governor is also anti-abortion, albeit he supports exceptions for victims of rape or incest.

Background: In 2020, Louisiana voters approved a constitutional amendment saying that "a right to abortion and financing for abortion shall not be found in the Louisiana Constitution." 62 percent of the almost 2 million people who voted supported the change. Abortion was permitted in Louisiana until the 19th week of pregnancy. Following that, it was only authorized if the fetus would die anyhow or if continuing the pregnancy would endanger the mother's life or health.

The impact of the Supreme Court decision: Louisiana has a trigger law that automatically prohibits abortions. There is no exception for rape or incestuous relationships. The only exception is if the lady is in grave danger of death or incapacity. Earlier this week, Democratic Gov. John Bel Edwards signed legislation modifying numerous aspects of the law and subjecting abortion providers to up to ten years in prison and fines of up to $100,000. According to Edwards' office, the statute allows for the use of emergency contraception "for victims of rape and incest prior to the time when a pregnancy may be clinically detected."

Edwards also signed legislation requiring doctors to report when a medication intended for abortion is being utilized for another medical purpose. It is now prohibited to offer abortion medications to a state resident "via mail-order, courier, or as a result of an online transaction."

As of Friday, Louisiana's three abortion facilities—in New Orleans, Baton Rouge, and Shreveport—were no longer providing abortions to patients and instead urged pregnant women who needed the operation to go to locations where it was still legal.

MAINE,

Political power: Democrats control both chambers of the Maine Legislature, which is currently in session. Democratic Gov. Janet Mills has committed to defending abortion rights, saying she will "fight with all I have to protect reproductive rights."

Background: In 1993, a Republican governor of Maine signed legislation safeguarding the right to abortion before a fetus is viable. After that, abortion is only legal if the woman's life or health is endangered, or if the pregnancy is no longer viable. In 2019, lawmakers repealed a physician-only restriction, which Mills signed into law, allowing nurse practitioners, physician assistants, and other medical professionals to perform abortions.

Nothing will change in Maine as a result of the Supreme Court's decision. Any attempt to outlaw abortions when legislators gather next year would face fierce opposition. However, abortion doctors predicted an influx of patients seeking abortions from states that ban the procedure.

Major changes are unlikely unless former Republican Gov. Paul LePage unseats Mills and Republicans take control of both houses of the Legislature in November. LePage, a Catholic who opposes abortion rights, has stated that it is up to politicians to address the abortion issue as they see fit.

MARYLAND

Political control: Democrats dominate Maryland's legislature, which enhanced abortion access last year by abolishing a restriction that only physicians may perform them and mandating most insurance plans to cover abortion services at no cost. In April, the legislature overrode Republican Gov. Larry Hogan's veto of the bill.

Background: Maryland law protects the right to abortion. In 1991, the state passed laws to protect abortion rights in the event that the Supreme Court restricted access. In 1992, voters supported the right with 62 percent of the vote. Maryland law prohibits abortion restrictions prior to viability. Maryland has no gestational restrictions. Professionals make the decision based on clinical standards of care after viability.

The Supreme Court's decision has no direct impact on Maryland law.

What comes next: Maryland's new law, which would allow trained nurse practitioners, nurse midwives, and physician assistants to perform abortions, is set to go into effect on July 1. However, state funding for training totaling $3.5 million is not due until fiscal year 2024. Hogan, whose time is limited, has indicated that he will not sanction the funds sooner. Some nurse practitioners, nurse midwives, and physician assistants have received medication abortion training and will be permitted to deliver such services beginning next month.

MASSACHUSETTS

Political control: Both the Democrats who control the Massachusetts legislature and the state's Republican governor favor abortion access, although their positions differ on specific topics.

Background: Massachusetts has had a difficult relationship with abortion, in part due to the tremendous influence of the Catholic Church, which is anti-abortion. Its influence has waned in recent years, and Massachusetts has emerged as a firm supporter of abortion rights. In 2018, the state repealed an 1845 abortion law that had not been enforced from its books in preparation for the conservative majority on the United States Supreme Court. Shortly afterward, Democratic state lawmakers fought with Republican Gov. Charlie Baker, who claims he supports abortion rights, over a move to codify abortion rights into state law, allowing abortions after 24 weeks of pregnancy in circumstances when the mother is in danger of miscarriage the child would not survive after birth, and lower the age at which women could seek an abortion without parental or guardian consent from 18 to 16. Over Baker's veto, lawmakers passed the bill, known as the Roe Act.

The impact of the Supreme Court decision: Baker has pledged to fight to keep abortion legal in Massachusetts, but this is his final year in office. Both Democratic gubernatorial candidates, state Sen. Abortion rights are supported by Sonia Chang-Diaz and Attorney General Maura Healey. Geoff Diehl, a Republican candidate, stated that he believes in "the obligation to save human life whenever and wherever feasible." Fellow Republican candidate Chris Doughty indicated that he would "not pursue any changes to our state's abortion laws."

It's unlikely that Massachusetts would restrict abortion rights. Baker signed an executive order on Friday prohibiting state agencies from assisting another state's investigation of individuals or businesses for seeking or providing reproductive health services that are legal in Massachusetts. The state will also refuse to help with extradition requests from states seeking criminal prosecution of such individuals. According to the Guttmacher Institute, which advocates for abortion rights, there were 47 abortion facilities in Massachusetts in 2017. With Roe v. Wade reversed, it's unclear how many people would go there from states that prohibit or limit abortion.

MICHIGAN

Political power: Michigan's legislature is dominated by Republicans who seek to ban or restrict abortion access, whilst the state's Democratic governor supports access.

Background: A dormant 1931 legislation in Michigan prohibits practically all abortions, but it hasn't been enforced since Roe v. Wade. The Act made it a crime to use an instrument or administer any substance with the intent of terminating a pregnancy unless it was absolutely necessary to save the woman's life. It makes no exceptions for rape or incestuous relationships. Planned Parenthood of Michigan initiated a lawsuit challenging Michigan's restriction, anticipating that Roe would be overturned. In May, a state judge suspended the bill, arguing it violated the state constitution. Democrats Gov. Gretchen Whitmer and Attorney General Dana Nessel praised the decision.

The impact of the Supreme Court decision: The injunction imposed in the Planned Parenthood lawsuit ensures that abortion does not become outlawed overnight. Planned Parenthood of Michigan and other supporters believe the verdict indicates the state's abortion rights will be protected. However, Nessel's office noted in a statement to The Associated Press that "given the existing cases, we cannot predict what the condition of abortion rights will be in Michigan" following Roe.

What comes next: Whitmer also filed a lawsuit asking the state Supreme Court to overturn the 91-year-old law. It has not yet acted. Abortion rights supporters in Michigan intend to put the issue on the ballot this fall. Their proposed constitutional amendment would grant women the right to make pregnancy-related decisions without interference, including abortion and other reproductive services like as birth control. To be on the November ballot, the Reproductive Freedom for All organization must collect around 425,000 valid voter signatures by July 11. If voters approve it, the bill will become law. The issue is also expected to have an impact on statewide elections Whitmer and Nessel are both up for reelection this fall and legislative campaigns.

MINNESOTA

Political power: The Minnesota Legislature is split on abortion issues. Republicans dominate the Senate, while Democrats control the House, but majorities in both chambers are narrow, so power will be up for grabs in the November elections. The majority of Democrats in Congress support abortion rights. While Tim Walz is governor, he has claimed that "no abortion restriction will ever become legislation." However, he will be challenged this year by Republican Scott Jensen, who is opposed to abortion rights.

Background: In Minnesota, abortion is legal up to the point of fetal viability, which occurs around the 24th week of pregnancy. The state imposes various restrictions, including a 24-hour waiting time with state-mandated counseling, the need that both parents be informed prior to a child getting an abortion, and abortions can only be performed by physicians.

The state Supreme Court concluded in 1995 that the state constitution maintains abortion rights, thus nothing will change immediately in Minnesota. If Republicans take control of both chambers, they may put a constitutional amendment on the ballot as early as 2024 to overturn the ruling, but it's unclear if they will go that route.

Minnesota governors cannot veto constitutional amendments. However, amendments are difficult to pass since they require the support of the majority of people participating in the election, not just those voting for the amendment. Leaving the ballot blank is equivalent to voting "no."

Providers are bracing for an increase in women coming from other states to have abortions. Prior to the verdict, Sarah Stoesz, president and CEO of Planned Parenthood North Central States, stated that her organization was "fortifying" its delivery methods, including telemedicine. According to Dr. Sarah Traxler, the group's medical director, demand in Minnesota is likely to increase by up to 25%.

MISSISSIPPI

Political power: Republican Gov. Tate Reeves and Republican legislators in Mississippi have been trying for years to limit abortion access.

Background: Mississippi already had a statute prohibiting most abortions beyond 20 weeks, but the state's lone abortion facility only performed the operation until 16 weeks. In 2018, the state attempted to put into effect a bill that would make most abortions after 15 weeks illegal. That legislation served as the foundation for the litigation that the Supreme Court is currently using to overturn Roe v. Wade. Mississippi's 15-week legislation was barred from taking effect in 2018, and an appeals court agreed. The Supreme Court agreed to consider the case in 2021. In December, the Supreme Court heard arguments, with the Mississippi attorney general's office urging the court to overturn Roe v. Wade. Mississippi has one abortion clinic, which closes at 16 weeks. Reeves served as Mississippi's lieutenant governor in 2018, when the state attempted to impose the 15-week limit, and in 2019, when the state attempted to enact a six-week restriction. Mississippi law prohibits physicians from providing abortion drugs via telemedicine consultations.

The Jackson Women's Health Organization, Mississippi's lone abortion clinic, is set to close in early July unless a judge overturns a trigger legislation. The clinic filed a lawsuit on Monday, challenging a 2007 legislation that would make most abortions illegal if Roe v. Wade were overturned. The bill is set to go into force on July 7. Abortions would still be permitted if the pregnancy endangers the woman's life or if the pregnancy was caused by a rape that was reported to law enforcement. Anyone, excluding the pregnant woman, who willfully performs or attempts to induce an abortion faces up to ten years in prison.

Under Mississippi law, the state attorney general is required to publish a notice in a state administrative bulletin after the United States Supreme Court overturns Roe v. Wade. Mississippi's ban on most abortions will go into effect 10 days after it is published.

MISSOURI

Political power: Both Republican Gov. Mike Parson and the Republican-led Legislature support abortion restrictions.

Previously, abortions up to 22 weeks of pregnancy were legal in Missouri. However, a 2019 state law prohibited abortions "unless in instances of medical necessity" if the United States Supreme Court overturned its 1973 Roe v. Wade decision. Under that Missouri act, illegal abortion is a criminal punishable by 5 to 15 years in prison, but women who have abortions are not punished.

The 2019 law includes a provision that makes it effective upon notification by the attorney general, governor, or Legislature that the United States Supreme Court has overruled Roe v. Wade. Attorney General Eric Schmitt and Missouri Gov. Mike Parson filed the necessary paperwork shortly after the Supreme Court's decision on Friday. The state legislation was subsequently updated online on Friday, indicating that the abortion-ban statute had gone into force.

Abortion-seekers in Missouri are anticipated to go to neighboring states such as Illinois and Kansas. A new Illinois logistics center in St. Louis helps out-of-state women find transportation, hotels, and childcare if they need assistance coming to the area for an abortion, and it connects them with financial sources. In 2019, the Kansas Supreme Court ruled that access to abortion is a "fundamental" right guaranteed by the state constitution. Even without the Missouri limitation, the number of Missouri patients seeking abortions in Kansas has increased in recent years, increasing by roughly 8% between 2020 and 2021.

MONTANA

Republicans in charge of the Montana Legislature, as well as Republican Gov. Greg Gianforte, want to restrict abortion access.

Background: Abortion was formerly legal in Montana up to viability, or around 24 weeks of pregnancy, but the state Legislature reduced it to 20 weeks in 2021, claiming that is when the fetus can feel pain. This legislation, as well as one requiring chemical abortions to be performed under the supervision of a physician, are being challenged in court. A state judge has temporarily postponed enforcement until October 2021 until the legal objections are resolved. The state has asked the Montana Supreme Court to overturn a 1999 Montana Supreme Court decision that determined the state's constitutional right to privacy ensures a woman's access to abortion services.

The impact of the Supreme Court decision is undetermined due to the ongoing legal challenges against the 2021 state law. Montana does not have an abortion ban that became effective when Roe v. Wade was overturned, but the Legislature may seek to severely restrict access in the future session.

What comes next: The Montana Supreme Court will rule on the preliminary injunction. The Montana Legislature also allowed a referendum in November to ask voters if they support a state law requiring abortion providers to provide lifesaving care to a fetus born alive after a botched abortion. Opponents argue that federal law already provides those safeguards.

NEBRASKA

Political control: Nebraska has a nominally nonpartisan legislature with a Republican majority but no supermajority that would allow the party to impose an abortion ban unilaterally. Democrats appear to have enough votes to block such a scheme, but a single defector might tip the vote. Nebraska's Republican governor is vehemently opposed to abortion.

Background: Most abortions in Nebraska are legal until the 22nd week of pregnancy, but a few small communities have elected to restrict the procedure inside their borders. When patients take the first of two drugs used in medication abortions, the law requires doctors to be physically present. Legislators have rejected plans to allow abortion medications to be administered remotely, which would increase abortion access in rural areas.

Effect of Supreme Court decision: A finding that allows states to determine their own abortion restrictions would prompt an immediate attempt by Nebraska conservatives to prohibit the procedure, though it's unclear if they'd be successful this year. Unlike other conservative states, Nebraska does not have a trigger law that prohibits abortion immediately. Gov. Pete Ricketts and other top Republicans have stated that a special legislative session will be called, but it is unclear if they will have the numbers to pass anything.

If Ricketts calls a special session, the spotlight would likely shift to state Sen. Justin Wayne, an Omaha Democrat who has yet to clarify his position on abortion. Wayne was conspicuously absent from a vote on the issue this year; his support would provide Republicans with the supermajority required to enact a ban. In the past, he has reached agreements with senators from both parties. If a proposed abortion ban fails during a special session, or if no special session is called, the issue will very certainly become a campaign issue in November.

Political power: Michigan's legislature is dominated by Republicans who seek to ban or restrict abortion access, while the state's Democratic governor supports access.

A dormant 1931 law in Michigan prohibits practically all abortions, but it hasn't been enforced since Roe v. Wade. The Act made it a crime to use an instrument or administer any substance with the intent of terminating a pregnancy unless it was absolutely necessary to save the woman's life. It makes no exceptions for rape or incestuous relationships. Planned Parenthood of Michigan initiated a lawsuit challenging Michigan's restrictions, anticipating that Roe would be overturned. In May, a state judge suspended the bill, arguing it violated the state constitution. Democratic Gov. Gretchen Whitmer and Attorney General Dana Nessel praised the decision.

The impact of the Supreme Court decision: The injunction imposed in the Planned Parenthood lawsuit ensures that abortion does not become outlawed overnight. Planned Parenthood of Michigan and other supporters believe the verdict indicates the state's abortion rights will be protected. However, Nessel's office noted in a statement to The Associated Press that "given the existing cases, we cannot predict what the condition of abortion rights will be in Michigan" following Roe.

What comes next: Whitmer also filed a lawsuit asking the state Supreme Court to overturn the 91-year-old law. It has not yet acted. Abortion rights supporters in Michigan intend to put the issue on the ballot this fall. Their proposed constitutional amendment would grant women the right to make pregnancy-related decisions without interference, including abortion and other reproductive services like birth control. To be on the November ballot, the Reproductive Freedom for All organization must collect around 425,000 valid voter signatures by July 11. If voters approve it, the bill will become law. The issue is also expected to have an impact on statewide elections. Whitmer and Nessel are both up for reelection this fall and have legislative campaigns.

MINNESOTA,

Political power: The Minnesota Legislature is split on abortion issues. Republicans dominate the Senate, while Democrats control the House, but majorities in both chambers are narrow, so power will be up for grabs in the

November elections. The majority of Democrats in Congress support abortion rights. While Tim Walz is governor, he has claimed that "no abortion restriction will ever become legislation." However, he will be challenged this year by Republican Scott Jensen, who is opposed to abortion rights.

Background: In Minnesota, abortion is legal up to the point of fetal viability, which occurs around the 24th week of pregnancy. The state imposes various restrictions, including a 24-hour waiting time with state-mandated counseling, the need for both parents to be informed prior to a child getting an abortion, and abortions can only be performed by physicians.

The state Supreme Court concluded in 1995 that the state constitution maintains abortion rights, so nothing will change immediately in Minnesota. If Republicans take control of both chambers, they may put a constitutional amendment on the ballot as early as 2024 to overturn the ruling, but it's unclear if they will go that route. Minnesota governors cannot veto constitutional amendments. However, amendments are difficult to pass since they require the support of the majority of people participating in the election, not just those voting for the amendment. Leaving the ballot blank is equivalent to voting "no."

Providers are bracing for an increase in women coming from other states to have abortions. Prior to the verdict, Sarah Stoesz, president and CEO of Planned Parenthood North Central States, stated that her organization was "fortifying" its delivery methods, including telemedicine. According to Dr. Sarah Traxler, the group's medical director, demand in Minnesota is likely to increase by up to 25%.

MISSISSIPPI

Republican Gov. Tate Reeves and Republican legislators in Mississippi have been trying for years to limit abortion access.

Background: Mississippi already had a statute prohibiting most abortions beyond 20 weeks, but the state's lone abortion facility only performed the operation until 16 weeks. In 2018, the state attempted to put into effect a bill that would make most abortions after 15 weeks illegal. That legislation served as the foundation for the litigation that the Supreme Court is currently using to overturn Roe v. Wade. Mississippi's 15-week legislation was barred from taking effect in 2018, and an appeals court agreed. The Supreme Court agreed in 2021 to hear the case. In December, the Supreme Court heard arguments with the Mississippi attorney general's office urging the court to overturn Roe v. Wade. Mississippi has one abortion clinic, which closes at 16 weeks. Reeves served as Mississippi's lieutenant governor in 2018, when the state attempted to impose the 15-week limit, and in 2019, when the state attempted to enact a six-week restriction. Mississippi law prohibits physicians from providing abortion drugs via telemedicine consultations.

The Jackson Women's Health Organization, Mississippi's lone abortion clinic, is set to close in early July unless a judge overturns trigger legislation. The clinic filed a lawsuit on Monday, challenging a 2007 law that would make most abortions illegal if Roe v. Wade were overturned. The bill is set to go into force on July 7. Abortions would still be permitted if the pregnancy endangers the woman's life or if the pregnancy was caused by a rape that was reported to law enforcement. Anyone, excluding the pregnant woman, who willfully performs or attempts to induce an abortion faces up to ten years in prison.

Under Mississippi law, the state attorney general is required to publish a notice in a state administrative bulletin after the United States Supreme Court overturns Roe v. Wade. Mississippi's ban on most abortions will go into effect 10 days after it is published.

MISSOURI

Both Republican Gov. Mike Parson and the Republican-led Legislature support abortion restrictions.

Previously, abortions up to 22 weeks of pregnancy were legal in Missouri. However, a 2019 state law prohibited abortions "unless in instances of medical necessity" if the United States Supreme Court overturned its 1973 Roe v. Wade decision. Under that Missouri act, illegal abortion is a crime punishable by 5 to 15 years in prison, but women who have abortions are not punished.

The 2019 law includes a provision that makes it effective upon notification by the attorney general, governor, or legislature that the United States Supreme Court has overruled Roe v. Wade. Missouri Attorney General Eric Schmitt and Missouri Gov. Mike Parson filed the necessary paperwork shortly after the Supreme Court's decision on Friday. The state legislation was subsequently updated online on Friday, indicating that the abortion-ban statute had gone into force.

Abortion-seekers in Missouri are anticipated to go to neighboring states such as Illinois and Kansas. A new Illinois logistics center in St. Louis helps out-of-state women find transportation, hotels, and childcare if they need assistance coming to the area for an abortion, and it connects them with financial sources. In 2019, the Kansas Supreme Court ruled that access to abortion is a "fundamental" right guaranteed by the state constitution. Even without the Missouri limitation, the number of Missouri patients seeking abortions in Kansas has increased in recent years, increasing by roughly 8% between 2020 and 2021.

MONTANA,

Republicans in charge of the Montana Legislature, as well as Republican Gov. Greg Gianforte, want to restrict abortion access.

Background: Abortion was formerly legal in Montana up to viability, or around 24 weeks of pregnancy, but the state Legislature reduced it to 20 weeks in 2021, claiming that is when the fetus can feel pain. This legislation, as well as one requiring chemical abortions to be performed under the supervision of a physician, is being challenged in court. A state judge has temporarily postponed enforcement until October 2021 until the legal objections are resolved. The state has asked the Montana Supreme Court to overturn a 1999 Montana Supreme Court decision that determined the state's constitutional right to privacy ensures a woman's access to abortion services.

The impact of the Supreme Court decision is undetermined due to the ongoing legal challenges against the 2021 state law. Montana does not have an abortion ban that became effective when Roe v. Wade was overturned, but the Legislature may seek to severely restrict access in the future session.

What comes next: The Montana Supreme Court will rule on the preliminary injunction. The Montana Legislature also allowed a referendum in November to ask voters if they support a state law requiring abortion providers to provide lifesaving care to a fetus born alive after a botched abortion. Opponents argue that federal law already provides those safeguards.

NEBRASKA

Political control: Nebraska has a nominally nonpartisan legislature with a Republican majority but no supermajority that would allow the party to impose an abortion ban unilaterally. Democrats appear to have enough votes to block such a scheme, but a single defector might tip the vote. Nebraska's Republican governor is vehemently opposed to abortion.

Background: Most abortions in Nebraska are legal until the 22nd week of pregnancy, but a few small communities have elected to restrict the procedure inside their borders. When patients take the first of two drugs used in medication abortions, the law requires doctors to be physically present. Legislators have rejected plans to allow abortion medications to be administered remotely, which would increase abortion access in rural areas.

A finding that allows states to determine their own abortion restrictions would prompt an immediate attempt by Nebraska conservatives to prohibit the procedure, though it's unclear if they'd be successful this year. Unlike other conservative states, Nebraska does not have a trigger law that prohibits abortion immediately. Gov. Pete Ricketts and other top Republicans have stated that a special legislative session will be called, but it is unclear if they will have the numbers to pass anything.

If Ricketts calls a special session, the spotlight would likely shift to state Sen. Justin Wayne, an Omaha Democrat who has yet to clarify his position on abortion. Wayne was conspicuously absent from a vote on the issue this year; his support would have provided Republicans with the supermajority required to enact a ban. In the past, he has reached agreements with senators from both parties. If a proposed abortion ban fails during a special session, or if no special session is called, the issue will very certainly become a campaign issue in November.

NEVADA

Political power: Nevada's governor and state attorney general are Democrats who are up for reelection this year. Democrats dominate the state Senate and Assembly.

Background: In 1990, Nevada voters enshrined the right to abortion in the state constitution. The law states that a pregnancy can be terminated within the first 24 weeks, and then only to save the pregnant woman's life or health. To change or repeal the act, another statewide vote would be required. The majority of Republican candidates for Congress, governor, state attorney general, and other statewide positions have stated their opposition to abortion.

"Here in Nevada, overturning Roe would not be felt immediately," state Attorney General Aaron Ford noted in a position statement prepared after the draft U.S. Supreme Court decision became public. Ford stated that a federal abortion ban would supersede state law and that it would be foolish not to recognize that some people want to restrict abortions or make them more difficult to obtain. However, he stated that his organization will fight "attacks on abortion rights, access to birth control, and rights for LGTBQ persons." In a statement, Gov. Steve Sisolak pledged to "continue to defend reproductive freedom."

Anti-abortion activists are unlikely to focus on overturning Nevada's abortion legislation. They will, however, seek regulations affecting waiting periods, mandatory therapy, or requiring parental knowledge or authorization. According to Melissa Clement, executive director of Nevada Right to Life, there is widespread support for parental involvement.

HAMPSHIRE, NEW

New Hampshire has a Republican governor, and Republicans dominate the 424-member Legislature. All are up for reelection this autumn.

Background: Any abortion restrictions in place in New Hampshire prior to Roe v. Wade were not enforced after the landmark 1973 decision, and they were repealed entirely in 1997. Until January, when the state enacted a law prohibiting abortion beyond 24 weeks of pregnancy. An exception was introduced in June for circumstances in when the fetus has "abnormalities incompatible with life." Anticipating the Supreme Court decision, Democrats attempted unsuccessfully this year to incorporate Abortion rights have been included into state legislation and the state constitution. Gov. Chris Sununu is pro-choice and says he is committed to upholding Roe v. Wade, but he also claims, "I've done more on the pro-life issue than anyone."

The Supreme Court's decision has no immediate impact in New Hampshire. The Legislature will not reconvene until September, when it will hold a one-day session to consider vetoed bills, and new legislation would require a two-thirds majority vote.

According to the majority leader of the New Hampshire House, the public should not anticipate Republicans in the Legislature to tighten state abortion rules any more. However, anti-abortion MPs who have already introduced legislation are expected to do so again.

NEW JERICHO

Democrats control both chambers of the state legislature as well as the governorship. Gov. Phil Murphy began his second consecutive term in office this year.

Background: Murphy campaigned for reelection on the promise that he would sign legislation enshrining abortion rights in state law, which he did in January. The Act also guaranteed the right to contraception as well as the right to carry a pregnancy to term. It stopped short of requiring abortion insurance coverage, as advocates had hoped. Instead, it empowers the state Banking and Insurance Department to conduct research and, if necessary, draft legislation. State payments to women's clinics, including Planned Parenthood, were reduced under Murphy's predecessor, Republican Chris Christie. Murphy reinstated them and has been a vocal supporter of abortion rights. There are no significant restrictions on abortion in New Jersey, such as parental consent or a required waiting period.

Effect of Supreme Court decision: Officials, including the governor, have stated that the repeal of Roe v. Wade would not result in a reduction in abortion services in the state. "Instead of hoping for the best, we prepared for the worse," Murphy said in May, responding to worries about a leaked copy of a Supreme Court decision.

Murphy has proposed a slew of abortion-related measures. On the Monday after the ruling, the Legislature began debating a pair of bills to expand abortion rights. One would allow the state to prohibit the extradition of someone facing a criminal charge in another state in connection with legally obtained reproductive services in New Jersey. Another states that out-of-state citizens may obtain abortion services in New Jersey, as well as allowing anyone facing liability judgments stemming from abortion services to suit in court.

MEXICO NEW YORK

Political control: The Democrats who dominate the New Mexico Legislature support access to abortion, as does the state's Democratic governor. Several conservative Democratic state senators who voted against repealing the abortion ban in 2019 were defeated in the 2020 primary by more socially progressive candidates.

Background: In 2021, state lawmakers repealed a dormant 1969 legislation that classified most abortions as felonies, ensuring access to abortion even after the federal court lifted guarantees. Albuquerque is home to one of just a few independent clinics in the country that perform third-trimester abortions without restrictions. An abortion clinic in Santa Teresa, New Mexico, is less than a mile from the Texas border and serves patients from El Paso, western Texas, and Arizona.

The Supreme Court's decision will have no immediate impact on New Mexico now that Roe v. Wade has been overturned. It is unclear if Democrats, who control the state Legislature, would seek stronger guarantees of abortion access when lawmakers convene in January. Legislative reform options include enshrining abortion rights in the state constitution, which would require voter approval. Abortion rights advocates say that the state's equal rights amendment might be used to divert more public funds to abortion-related activities. Ral Torrez, the district attorney in Albuquerque and a Democratic candidate for attorney general, is urging Congress to take more steps to ensure abortion access, including safeguards for women traveling from adjacent states. The state Republican Party believes it is time to elect more anti-abortion legislators.

What's next: The state should expect a constant influx of people seeking abortions from neighboring states with stricter abortion regulations. It already serves patients from Texas and Oklahoma, which last year enacted some of the most stringent abortion restrictions in the country.

United States Of America

Political control: The Democrats who control the New York Legislature, as well as the state's Democratic governor, favor abortion rights.

Background: Abortion has been legal in New York since 1970, when a measure passed by the Republican-controlled Legislature and signed by Republican Gov. Nelson A. Rockefeller was passed. Abortions are legal within the first 24 weeks of pregnancy or to save the mother's life. The 2019 Reproductive Health Act decriminalized abortion, codified Roe v. Wade, and legalized abortions after 24 weeks if a fetus isn't viable or to save the mother's life or health. In New York, lawmakers have passed legislation that strengthens legal protections for those seeking and conducting abortions.

Roe v. Wade safeguards are implemented into state law as a result of the Supreme Court decision. New York plans to spend $35 million this year on abortion facilities to improve services and bolster security in anticipation of a surge of out-of-state women seeking abortions after the ruling is issued. It's unclear how many more individuals from neighboring states will come to New York for abortion care. According to the Guttmacher Institute, a research organization that advocates for abortion rights, New York has 252 abortion facilities in 2017.

Planned Parenthood and civil rights organizations are urging lawmakers to begin the process of seeking a constitutional amendment to protect access to abortion care in the event that the present legislation is repealed by a future Legislature.

NORTHEAST CAROLINA

Republicans hold a majority in the state House and Senate, but not enough to override a veto by Democratic Gov. Roy Cooper, an outspoken supporter of abortion rights. Cooper has vetoed a "born-alive" abortion measure as well as a law prohibiting abortion based on race or a Down syndrome diagnosis since 2017. Due to term limits, he cannot run for reelection in 2024.

Background: A 1973 North Carolina legislation that prohibited most abortions after 20 weeks of pregnancy is now unenforceable after federal judges ruled it illegal in 2019 and 2021. Abortions can instead be performed until fetal viability. A state law passed in 2015 restricted post-viability abortions to "medical emergencies," implying the woman would die or face a "serious risk" of significant and irreversible bodily damage without the procedure.

The 20-week ban may be reinstated now that Roe v. The Supreme Court has reversed Wade. According to legal experts, formal action would be required to overturn the previous court orders. Republican legislative leaders asked state Attorney General Josh Stein, a Democrat and abortion rights champion whose office defended the 20-week measure, to act late Friday. Otherwise, they stated that they would try to intervene.

Republican General Assembly leaders do not expect to discuss additional abortion restrictions during the soon-to-end legislative session, implying that the GOP's electoral efforts to secure the five additional seats required to achieve veto-proof margins in 2023 will likely be accelerated. Cooper and other Democrats have already made abortion rights a central campaign issue. Abortion politics are also expected to play a role in the November elections for two state Supreme Court seats. If Republicans win at least one of these, they will have a majority on the court.

DAKOTA, NORTH

Political control: North Dakota's legislature is dominated by Republicans who want to restrict abortion, and the Republican governor wanted Roe v. Wade repealed in favor of state rights.

Background: The state has enacted some of the most stringent abortion restrictions in the country, including one that would have prohibited abortions if a fetal heartbeat could be detected, This can occur before a woman is aware she is pregnant. The measure was never implemented because the state's sole abortion provider successfully challenged it in court. One Republican bill that was defeated would have charged abortion providers with murder, with a possible life sentence.

North Dakota has introduced legislation that would down the state's lone abortion facility in Fargo after 30 days as a result of the Supreme Court verdict. That 2007 state legislation makes abortion illegal unless it is necessary to save the pregnant woman's life or in cases of rape or incest. Violators might face a five-year prison sentence and a $10,000 fine.

The owner and operator of the Red River Women's Clinic in Fargo stated that she will investigate all legal options to ensure that abortion services are available in North Dakota. If that fails, clinic leader Tammi Kromenaker plans to relocate over the river to Moorhead, Minnesota, where abortion is not illegal. Planned Parenthood claims it can deliver abortions in Moorhead until Kromenaker gets up and running.

OHIO

Political control: The Ohio Legislature is controlled by Republicans who advocate limiting or prohibiting abortions, and the Republican governor backs similar efforts. This year, he is fighting for reelection against a former mayor who supports abortion rights.

Prior to Friday's decision, Ohio did not prohibit most abortions until the 22nd week of pregnancy; beyond that, they are only permitted to save a patient's life or when their health is significantly compromised. However, the state imposes a number of other restrictions, including parental clearance for minors, an ultrasound requirement, and in-person counseling followed by a 24-hour waiting period. Abortions on the basis of fetal Down syndrome are prohibited. Ohio also restricts state funding for abortions to cases of rape, incest, or imminent danger to the patient's life. It restricts abortion-related insurance coverage for public workers as well as coverage via health plans marketed in the Affordable Care Act health market to the same circumstances. A number of rules must be followed by abortion clinics.

The impact of the Supreme Court decision: A ban on most abortions at the first detected fetal heartbeat became law in Ohio hours after the judgement. The implementation of Ohio's 2019 "heartbeat" ban has been halted for nearly three years due to a federal court order. Because of the high court's decision, the state attorney general, Republican Dave Yost, requested that it be dissolved, and U.S. Judge Michael Barrett agreed hours later.

Two trigger proposals remain on hold in the Legislature, but a top parliamentary leader has said that if the judgement is reversed, new legislation that more clearly represents the true result will be required. That would almost certainly not happen until MPs returned to the capital following the November election.

Activists are looking on ways to help Ohioans seeking abortions abroad. They may even stage a statewide referendum initiative to enshrine abortion rights in the state constitution, though this is unlikely to happen until next year. Abortion opponents are considering ways to secure a statewide abortion ban.

OKLAHOMA

Political control: Republicans in Oklahoma have a supermajority in both chambers of the Legislature and a Republican governor who has pledged to support "any pro-life initiative that comes over my desk."

Background: Abortion services in Oklahoma were banned in May after Gov. Kevin Stitt signed legislation outlawing all abortions with a few exceptions. Civil litigation, rather than criminal punishment, is used to enforce the prohibition. According to the Guttmacher Institute, Republican legislators have been fighting for decades to limit abortion in the state, enacting 81 different restrictions since Roe v. Wade was founded in 1973.

The Supreme Court's decision will have little practical impact because abortions are no longer available in Oklahoma. Oklahoma similarly had a "trigger legislation" that made abortion illegal as soon as Roe was overturned.

Given the governor's and Legislature's staunch opposition to abortion, Oklahoma will continue to restrict the practice if states are given the ability to do so. Meanwhile, abortion doctors who previously practiced in the state are making efforts to assist patients in seeking abortions outside of the state, such as arranging financing for these women and establishing a referral network of therapists to assist with difficulties before or after a woman obtains an abortion.

OREGON

Political power: The Democrats who control the Oregon Legislature, as well as the state's Democratic governor, favor abortion rights.

Background: In 1969, the Oregon Legislature passed legislation legalizing abortion. Gov. Kate Brown passed legislation in 2017 expanding health care coverage for reproductive services, including abortions, to thousands of Oregonians regardless of poverty, citizenship status, or gender identity. Oregon has no substantial abortion restrictions, and abortion is legal at any stage of pregnancy.

The Guttmacher Institute predicts that Oregon will experience a 234 percent increase in women seeking abortions from out of state, primarily from Idaho, as a result of the Supreme Court decision. Oregon lawmakers appropriated $15 million in March to expand abortion access and pay for abortions as well as support services such as travel and lodging for both local and out-of-state patients.

Brown indicated following the announcement of the draft Supreme Court judgment that access to abortion is a basic right and that she will strive to ensure that access to abortion is protected by state law in Oregon. Democratic state legislators have formed the Reproductive Health and Access to Care Work Group, which includes physicians, clinics, community organizations, and politicians, and will provide recommendations for the 2023 parliamentary session and beyond. Recommendations may include safeguarding, improving, and expanding equitable access to all sorts of reproductive care.

The trigger law, which prohibits practically all abortions, went into force Friday evening, when the parliamentary general counsel communicated the Supreme Court judgement to legislators. It does offer limited exceptions for rape and incest if the offenses are reported to law enforcement, as well as severe risk to the mother's life or health, as well as known lethal birth defects.

Under Utah law, performing an abortion is a crime punishable by up to 15 years in jail and a $10,000 fine. While it is primarily aimed at providers, politicians have recognized that a woman who self-administers an abortion, including with medication, may face criminal charges.

VERMONT

Political control: Democrats dominate the Vermont Legislature, despite Republican Gov. Phil Scott's staunch support for abortion rights.

Background: Vermont has enacted laws guaranteeing the right to abortion in 2019, and voters will discuss a proposal to amend the state constitution to protect abortion rights in November. Also in 2019, the Vermont Legislature initiated the Reproductive Liberty Amendment, or Proposition 5, process to amend the state constitution to protect abortion rights. The word "abortion" is not used in Vermont's proposed amendment. Proponents claim that this is because it is intended to preserve other reproductive rights, such as the freedom to get pregnant or acquire birth control. Opponents say that vague language might have unanticipated consequences that could last for years. In February, lawmakers approved the proposed amendment, paving the path for a statewide vote.

The Supreme Court's decision has no direct impact on Vermont.

In November, Vermont voters will decide whether to amend the state's constitution to protect abortion rights.

VIRGINIA

Political control: Virginia has a Republican governor who has shown his support for increased state-level abortion restrictions. Gov. Glenn Youngkin said Friday that he will introduce legislation to prohibit most abortions after 15 weeks. Youngkin told The Washington Post that he had asked four anti-abortion Republican legislators to work on the legislation. He told the Post that a 20-week moratorium may be necessary to achieve unanimity in Virginia's divided legislature, where Republicans control the House and Democrats control the Senate. Youngkin often advocates exceptions to abortion laws in cases of rape, incest, or when the mother's life is in danger.

Background: During Democrats' entire control of the state government in recent years, lawmakers relaxed abortion regulations. They repealed strict building code controls on abortion facilities, as well as requirements that a patient seeking an abortion undergo a 24-hour waiting period and an ultrasound. Proponents believed that the revisions would make Virginia a safe haven for abortion access in the South. The Republican triumph in the November elections changed the political landscape in the state, although Senate Democrats defeated multiple bills that would have restricted abortion access during the 2022 legislative session.

The Supreme Court's decision will have no immediate impact on abortion rules in Virginia now that Roe v. Wade has been overturned. Some abortion providers predict an influx of patients seeking care in Virginia from neighboring states that have "trigger laws" restricting abortion.

The future of abortion access in Virginia is uncertain. Senate Democrats say they will continue to oppose efforts to limit abortion access, but they control the chamber by the slimmest of margins and have one caucus member who personally opposes abortion and says he is open to greater restrictions. Republicans also retain a tenuous majority in the House, with few moderate members. In 2023, every member of the General Assembly will be up for election.

WASHINGTON

Political control: The Democrats who control the Washington legislature, as well as the state's Democratic governor, favor abortion rights.

Background: Abortion has been legal in Washington state since a statewide ballot referendum in 1970. Another ballot item supported by voters in 1991 established a woman's right to choose physician-assisted abortion prior to fetal viability and increased and safeguarded abortion access in the state if Roe v. Wade was reversed. In 2018, the Legislature passed legislation requiring Washington insurers that provide maternity care to cover elective abortions and contraception. Gov. Jay Inslee approved legislation earlier this year that allows physician assistants, advanced registered nurse practitioners, and other professionals practicing within their scope of practice to perform abortions. Supporters argue that the change is intended to help fulfill the demand from an inflow of out-of-state patients. The same law forbids Washington state from taking legal action against people seeking abortions and those who assist them.

The state "will deploy every available instrument to secure and sustain Washingtonians' basic freedom to choose, as well as protect the rights of anybody who wants to come here to get reproductive health care," said Democrat Attorney General Bob Ferguson. According to data from the Washington State Department of Health, 852 of the 16,909 abortions conducted in the state that year included non-residents. The bulk of them were from adjacent states like Idaho and Oregon.

While it's hard to anticipate how many additional non-resident patients may seek care in Washington now that Roe v. Wade has been reversed, Jennifer Allen, CEO of Planned Parenthood Alliance Advocates, believes the rise will be in the hundreds. The state contains more than 30 abortion facilities, the great majority of which are located in western Washington around the Interstate 5 corridor.

VIRGINIA, WEST

West Virginia's legislature is controlled by Republicans who seek to outlaw or restrict abortion access. Republican Gov. Jim Justice opposes abortion access and has signed two anti-abortion bills since taking office in 2017.

Background: Currently, abortion after the 20th week of pregnancy is illegal in West Virginia unless the patient's life is in danger or they suffer "severe and permanent physical impairment of a significant bodily function." Patients seeking abortions must wait 24 hours after receiving legally mandated abortion-dissuasion counseling. A minor who wishes to get an abortion must have parental consent. It is prohibited to utilize telemedicine to administer a pharmacological abortion. The law also prohibits people from obtaining abortions because they believe their child will be born with a disability. This year, the House of Delegates passed a 15-week abortion ban, but it was defeated in the Senate.

The impact of the Supreme Court decision: It is unknown what impact the decision will have on abortion access in West Virginia. Since 1848, the state has had abortion laws on the books; under that law, practitioners who perform abortions risk criminal charges and three to ten years in prison, unless the abortion is performed to save a patient's life. West Virginia voters approved a constitutional amendment in 2018 declaring that patients do not have the right to abortion and prohibiting public financing for abortions.

When lawmakers return to the Capitol in January, they may introduce new legislation restricting abortion access, although they might return sooner if called into a special session. There is just one abortion clinic in West Virginia. If abortion access is restricted, the Women's Health Center of West Virginia, according to Executive Director Katie Quinonez, will continue to provide reproductive care, including birth control and STI screening and treatment. She added that the clinic will use its abortion fund to help women fly to other states for abortions.

WISCONSIN

Political power: Wisconsin has a Republican-controlled legislature that wants to ban or restrict abortion access but a Democratic governor who supports access and is up for reelection this year.

Background: Wisconsin has allowed most abortions until the 22nd week of pregnancy in order to save the woman's health or life. A woman seeking an abortion must speak with a counselor and doctor before obtaining an abortion and wait at least 24 hours before having it done. Anyone under age 18 must have an adult relative over age 25 accompany them to have an abortion.

Now that Roe v. Wade has been overturned, it is possible that a state law passed in 1849 declaring abortion a criminal offense may go into force, and physicians have stopped performing abortions. However, Wisconsin's Democratic attorney general claims that the act is invalid because it is so old. The phrase allows a woman to legally terminate her own pregnancy or embryo and also provides protection if an abortion is required to preserve a woman's life and is performed in a hospital. Another state legislation, passed in 1985, prohibits abortions after a fetus reaches viability, or the point at which it may survive outside the womb, contradicting the 1849 restriction. order to ensure that a restriction remains in place, even as the issue is being litigated in court. However, if Democratic Gov. Tony Evers is re-elected, lawmakers' efforts would be impeded. Wisconsin Republican Assembly Speaker Robin Vos has stated that he supports a rape exception and that a Roe decision may require lawmakers to address other pertinent reproductive issues like as contraception. Other Republicans will seek for even harsher abortion restrictions.

WYOMING

Political control: Wyoming has one of the most Republican legislatures in the country, with a strong history of libertarian-style conservatism, albeit not always social or religious conservatism. That might be changing. In March, Republican Gov. Mark Gordon signed into law a bill that would prohibit abortion in practically all circumstances should the Supreme Court reverse Roe v. Wade.

Background: Wyoming law now allows abortions until a fetus can survive on its own outside of its mother's body. The statute does not specify when this occurs, although it is generally assumed to occur about 23 weeks into pregnancy. Wyoming currently prohibits abortions after that point unless the woman is in grave danger of losing her life or health. Wyoming Republicans have always had a hands-off approach to abortion, but they have recently shown a willingness to regulate the process. Democrats in the legislature have declined from 26 in 2010 to only nine out of 90 total members now. A 2021 legislation mandates physicians to offer lifesaving care to any aborted fetus born alive. The new state legislation that forbids abortion only allows exceptions in cases of rape or incest, or to save the mother's life or health, and does not take psychological disorders into account. Abortions continue to take place despite the fact that

Wyoming has no abortion clinics. According to state officials, 98 took place in Wyoming in 2021.

PENNSYLVANIA

Republican dominance of the Pennsylvania legislature is opposed to abortion rights, but the state's Democratic governor is a strong supporter who has vetoed three GOP-drafted bills in five years that would have expanded restrictions beyond the state's 24-week limit. This year's governor's race might tip the scales.

Background: Abortion has been legal in Pennsylvania for decades, including a 1989 act that was challenged all the way to the United States Supreme Court. This resulted in the landmark Planned Parenthood v. Casey case, which upheld the Supreme Court's 1973 ruling in Roe v. Wade, which legalized abortion worldwide but also allowed states to set some restrictions on abortion availability.

As an impact of the Supreme Court decision, Gov. Tom Wolf has pledged to keep abortion legal for the rest of his term, which ends in January. The state's Democratic attorney general, Josh Shapiro, who supports abortion rights, and Republican state Sen. Doug Mastriano, who advocates prohibiting abortion completely, are both running to succeed him. The Republican-controlled Legislature is expected to remain in place next year.

A bill to ban abortion after the confirmation of a baby's heartbeat, which can occur as early as six weeks, before many women realize they are pregnant, has passed a House committee and is awaiting a floor vote. The state Supreme Court is considering a lawsuit filed by Planned Parenthood and other abortion clinics in an attempt to invalidate a 1982 law that prohibits the use of public funds for abortion except in cases of rape, incest, or to save the mother's life. In response, Republican lawmakers have suggested an amendment declaring that there is no constitutional right to abortion in Pennsylvania, nor is there any public funding for abortion.

RIVER ISLAND

Political power: The Democrats who control Rhode Island's General Assembly, as well as the Democratic governor, favor abortion rights.

Background: In 2019, Rhode Island's governor approved legislation to enshrine abortion safeguards in the event that the United States Supreme Court overturns its 1973 Roe v. Wade decision. The Act states that the state will not restrict the right to an abortion before fetal viability or later if necessary to save the pregnant woman's health or life. It repealed previous laws that had been deemed unconstitutional by the courts. The Rhode Island Supreme Court upheld the 2019 law in May, only two days after a draft ruling from the Supreme Court was leaked, indicating that a majority of the justices were poised to overturn Roe. Proponents of abortion have claimed that the measure breaches the state constitution. According to the state health department, there were 2,611 abortions in Rhode Island in 2020.

The 2019 Reproductive Privacy Act, according to Rhode Island's attorney general, will continue to ensure abortion access. Vote for Planned Parenthood! Because the right to abortion is entrenched in state law, Rhode Island has signaled that it will remain legal regardless of the ruling.

On the Monday after the Supreme Court decision, Rhode Island's Democratic governor stated that he will sign an executive order shielding the state's abortion providers from legal action by anti-abortion activists in other states. McKee's office did not provide a timeline for the signing, but stated that the governor intended to act as soon as possible. Secretary of State Nellie Gorbea and Matt Brown, McKee's Democratic primary opponents in September, had pressed him to issue such an order. They also want state lawmakers to return for a special session to add abortion coverage to Rhode Island's Medicaid program and state employee health insurance. Legislative leaders stated that abortion coverage would be addressed next year since it has financial implications and was not included in this year's budget.

DOWNEY, SOUTH CAROLINA

Political control: South Carolina has a Republican governor and a Republican-dominated General Assembly. However, if a Democrat wins the governorship in 2022, the party lacks the two-thirds majority in either chamber required to overcome procedural impediments or a veto.

Background: South Carolina passed the "Fetal Heartbeat and Protection from Abortion Act" in 2021, which requires practitioners to use an ultrasound to try to identify a fetal heartbeat if they think a pregnant woman is at least eight weeks along. If they find a heartbeat, they can only perform an abortion if the woman's life is in danger or the pregnancy is the result of rape or incest. The statute is now embroiled in federal litigation.

Following the Supreme Judge's decision to overturn Roe v. Wade, a federal court granted the state permission to begin enforcing the 2021 act. Planned Parenthood and others dropped their lawsuit, but the organization said it will continue to offer abortions in South Carolina under the new regulations.

The normal session of the South Carolina General Assembly concluded in May, but Republican leaders have pledged to return for a special session if the Supreme Court overturns Roe v. Wade. Despite Friday's decision, they have yet to call a special session. Some Republican leaders have opposed a total abortion ban, particularly one that excludes victims of rape and incest.

DAKOTA, SOUTH

Republicans hold supermajorities in both houses of the Statehouse. Kristi Noem, the Republican governor running for reelection this year, has been a vocal opponent of abortion rights.

Background: South Dakota now prohibits abortions beyond the 22nd week of pregnancy. There is just one abortion clinic in the state, a Planned Parenthood facility in Sioux Falls. Over the years, the legislature has attempted to make it more difficult for women to have abortions by establishing mandatory waiting periods and requiring them to study and sign papers discouraging them against terminating their pregnancies.

The impact of the Supreme Court decision: South Dakota has a trigger legislation that prohibits abortions unless the pregnant woman's life is in danger.

Noem has declared that if Roe v. Wade is overturned, she intends to call a special session to draft guidelines for the new legal environment. She has not commented on specific legislation, but lawmakers have discussed measures to make it more difficult for women to seek abortions outside of the state. South Dakota voters, however, rejected outright prohibitions in 2006 and 2008, and abortion rights activists are planning a similar referendum on abortion access. A total ban on abortions might be challenged in the future by a citizen-initiated ballot referendum.

TENNESSEE

Political power: Tennessee has a Republican governor who is outspoken in his opposition to abortion. The Republican Party holds a supermajority in the state legislature and has gradually reduced abortion access.

Background: In 2020, Tennessee adopted laws prohibiting most abortions after the fetal heartbeat can be detected at roughly six weeks, which is when many women are pregnant. Since it was quickly suspended by a federal judge, the bill has never been enforced. Tennessee voters approved an amendment in 2014 declaring that the state constitution does not protect or ensure the right to abortion or require the funding of abortions, and empowering state lawmakers to "enact, modify, or repeal laws concerning abortion." State law also prohibits physicians from providing abortion medicines via telemedicine consultations. Tennessee has six abortion facilities.

The impact of the Supreme Court's decision: Thirty days following the decision, so-called trigger legislation would take effect, prohibiting all abortions in Tennessee unless necessary to avert death or "serious threat of severe and permanent impairment of a key bodily function." Under this legislation, doctors who perform abortions may face criminal charges.

It's unclear if the trigger legislation would clash with the 2020 statute prohibiting most abortions after six weeks. The state's Republican attorney general has not publicly commented. Meanwhile, Republicans are expected to keep their supermajority after this year's midterm elections. Patients seeking abortions will be diverted to Illinois facilities if Roe v. Wade is overturned, or to Florida, where abortions will be limited to 15 weeks. Women in eastern Tennessee may have options in North Carolina and Virginia.

TEXAS

Political dominance: The Republican Party controls the Texas Legislature and has held every statewide position for nearly 30 years. Greg Abbott, a Republican, is up for reelection in November and is widely expected to win a third term.

Background: Texas has provided the nation with a glimpse of the landscape of abortion access in the absence of the Roe v. Wade protections. A new Texas law prohibiting most abortions after six weeks — before many women realize they are pregnant — went into effect in September and makes no exceptions for rape or incest. Texas has effectively outmaneuvered decades of Supreme Court precedent governing a woman's constitutional right to an abortion because of how Republicans drafted the law, which is only enforceable through lawsuits filed by private citizens against doctors or anyone who assists a woman in obtaining an abortion. According to state data, the number of abortions performed in Texas' nearly two dozen clinics fell by half in the five months following the law's implementation compared to the same period a year earlier.

The impact of the Supreme Court decision: Texas had more than 40 abortion facilities in 2012, before Republicans chipped away at abortion access for a decade, causing providers to close. Without Roe v. Wade, Texas intends to outlaw almost all abortions 30 days after the Supreme Court rules on the case, which could take about a month. Abortions would be legalized only if the patient's life was in danger or if they faced "substantial impairment of a significant bodily function."

Many Texas women have already flown out of state for abortions since the act went into force, but they will likely have to travel even further now that Roe has been overruled because other states prohibit abortion. Some Republican lawmakers also want to punish companies that assist their Texas-based employees in seeking abortions abroad, although it's uncertain how popular that idea would be when the Legislature reconvenes in 2023.

UTAH

Political control: Utah is a staunchly conservative state, with a Republican supermajority in the legislature.

For years, the state has restricted abortion, including a limitation after 18 weeks adopted in 2019 that is presently being challenged in court. The next year, lawmakers established a "trigger legislation" that would make almost all abortions illegal if Roe v. Wade was reversed.

A projected women's health clinic in Casper, which would have been the state's sole one offering abortions, was set to open in mid-June, but an arson incident on

May 25 pushed that date back by roughly six months. Despite the ruling, clinic founder Julie Burkhart said Friday that she still intends to open the clinic and will pursue legal methods to make abortion legal in Wyoming. The arson investigation is still ongoing, and police have offered a $5,000 reward for information leading to an arrest.

Chapter Three

ABORTION RIGHT IS WOMEN'S RIGHT

Abortion rights for women Too many women are still denied the right to choose their own destiny. They are denied access to abortion treatment in a safe environment.

An abortion is a relatively safe and simple medical technique for terminating a pregnancy. Aborting a pregnancy is a frequent decision that millions of people make each year. It is estimated that about one in every three pregnancies in the world ends in abortion.

Despite the widespread need for abortion across the world, access to safe and legal abortion services is far from guaranteed for those in need. This lack of access to abortion care has a negative impact on women's and pregnant people's fundamental rights to make informed decisions about their health and bodies.

Limiting abortion just makes it less safe.

While abortion is one of the safest medical procedures in the world, legislative and legal impediments continue to prevent women and pregnant people from receiving safe care.

According to research, actions to criminalize or restrict abortion access have little effect on the number of abortions performed. According to Guttmacher Institute data, abortion rates are virtually the same in countries where abortion is widely legal and in countries where it is not. Restricting access to healthcare services does not eliminate the demand, but rather drives women to seek hazardous services, putting their health and lives at danger.

When abortion is prohibited, it is typically existing marginalized populations who are most at risk and disproportionately affected, since they have few or no options for seeking safe and legal treatments in another nation or accessing private care if necessary. It is thought that nearly all unsafe abortions take place in the poor world, where nations with tight abortion restrictions are concentrated.

The Perils of Risky Abortion

The World Health Organization defines unsafe abortion as a procedure performed by someone who lacks the necessary expertise or in an environment that does not meet minimal medical standards, or both.

Almost half of all abortions worldwide are unsafe, with an estimated 35 million performed each year. According to data, seven million women will have problems, and over 22,000 women will die as a result of dangerous treatments. Unsafe abortions are responsible for 8–11 percent of maternal deaths worldwide.

In the 125 nations where abortion is strictly prohibited, 42 percent of women live.

What are the barriers to abortion access, and how may they be overcome?

While access to abortion care has improved considerably over the last two decades, we still see disparities in availability around the globe. Millions of women continue to face restrictions that limit their ability to choose whether and when to have children.

Excessive laws and over-medicalization frequently limit our services in every country where we work. This prevents people from seeking and receiving the help they so require. Access barriers might range from legal impediments to stigma, which causes women to prioritize concealment above safety.

Legal impediments to access

Abortion policies across the world range from absolute prohibition to abortion on demand. In 2017, 58 percent of women of reproductive age lived in nations where abortion was widely permitted. Despite this, 42 percent of women live in the 125 nations where abortion is severely prohibited.

There is still a long way to go until every woman has access to safe, legal abortion care. However, enormous progress is being made on a daily basis, and we know that public support for reproductive health is growing. In the United Kingdom, for example, 9 out of 10 people support abortion access. MSI is working with activists throughout the world to eliminate unnecessary governmental barriers to abortion, alongside a generation of young people who are more determined than ever to protect reproductive choice.

Social Barriers to Access

Even in places where abortion is mostly legal, there are still impediments to abortion care. Stigma and other harmful societal and cultural conventions can impede both women's ability to seek therapy and medical practitioners' willingness to give it.

Because of high levels of stigma and a culture of silence, women in need of safe services typically lack vital information about where to acquire them. For example, stigma might prevent women from sharing with their family or friends about their experience for fear of being judged, leaving many women feeling alienated and alone during and after their encounter. Quiet creates a stigma, and silence feeds misconceptions. Myths that misinform, mislead, and stigmatize We must break this vicious and fatal cycle.

Quiet creates a stigma, and silence feeds misconceptions. Myths that misinform, mislead, and stigmatize

Violation Of Civil Rights

(Washington, D.C.) — According to a draft opinion disclosed on Monday, a majority of Supreme Court justices are ready to overturn Roe v. Wade. If granted, the verdict will end federal constitutional protection for the right to abortion, allowing states to determine whether it is legal. While there is still a constitutionally protected right to abortion, the draft decision cautions that Roe v. Wade and decades of earlier Supreme Court rulings protecting the right are in grave danger of being overturned by the Court's conservative supermajority.

The Lawyers' Committee for Civil Rights Under Law, The Leadership Conference on Civil and Human Rights, and 16 other prominent civil rights groups filed an amicus brief in Dobbs v. Jackson Women's Health, the case under consideration in the leaked draft judgment, in September 2021. According to human rights organizations, Mississippi legislation prohibiting abortions beyond 15 weeks would disproportionately affect black women and women with low incomes.

Damon Hewitt, president and executive director of the Lawyers' Committee for Civil Rights Under Law, issued the following statement.

"By overturning Roe v. Wade, the Supreme Court has indicated its willingness to upend nearly fifty years of judicial precedent." This would be a tragic decision that, if made, would endanger all of us, particularly black women and women with little income. Individuals in disadvantaged groups are compelled to face problems that have a cascading effect on their health, economic well-being, and social position when abortion is banned. Abortion access is a matter of economic and racial fairness, as well as a critical component of civil rights. Reproductive freedom is a question of both bodily autonomy and self-determination. When people have the choice of whether, when, and how many children to have, they are able to make more deliberate decisions about other aspects of their lives, such as education and employment.

"The potential consequences of such a judgement jeopardize other aspects of the civil rights agenda that we have fought to advance for decades." By disregarding stare decisis, the legal premise that relies on earlier judgements, the Court jeopardizes the fundamental rights of millions of women and places our whole civil rights jurisprudence on shaky foundation. Other rights, based on Roe's understanding that the Bill of Rights provides marital, family, and sexual privacy, are now susceptible to the Court's judicial whims and scrutiny. A majority of justices is now poised to pull on a thread that has the potential to unravel our whole democracy.

"Justice Alito's draft judgment is especially remarkable in that it is based in part on his interpretation of centuries-old legal traditions from another country, going back to the Middle Ages." By viewing due process rights in this way, we risk reverting to a time when women, Black people, and other oppressed groups had no power, vote, or voice. It might serve as a continuous justification to codify discrimination and reject progress made by other historically oppressed people.

"Regardless of the challenges we encounter, the Lawyers' Committee remains committed to doing all possible to help codify the right to reproductive freedom." in law." We will continue to fight, agitate, and sue until we have built a society in which freedom, equality, and equity are fundamental to our legal system. We encourage Congress to do everything possible to pass the Women's Health Protection Act, which would protect women's access to abortions across the country. "The conflict is not over; it is just begun."

Background

Black women seek abortion therapy at a disproportionate rate due to bad state reproductive health policies such as limited sex education and a lack of health insurance and meaningful access to contraception and other reproductive health services. Furthermore, studies consistently show that access to abortion is linked to educational and economic advancement, and denial of that right can have substantial financial consequences for those affected.

The Lawyers' Committee for Civil Rights Under Law petitioned Congress in June 2021 to pass the Women's Health Protection Act, an all-inclusive health-care plan that would prohibit states from enacting medically unjustifiable abortion restrictions and prohibitions.

The Lawyers' Committee for Civil Rights Under Law (LCCRL) The Lawyers' Committee for Civil Rights Under Law (Lawyers' Committee) was founded in 1963 at the request of President John F. Kennedy to enlist the private bar in providing legal services to combat racial discrimination. The Lawyers' Committee for Civil Rights Under Law's primary objective is to establish equitable justice for everyone via the rule of law, notably in the areas of voting rights, Criminal justice, equitable housing and community development, economic fairness, educational opportunity, and hate crimes are all issues that must be addressed.

Chapter Four

ABORTION'S IN POST-ROE AMERICA

Roe v. Wade's demise will not put an end to abortion. This is what it will do. What happens to abortion in America if Roe v. Wade is overturned?

That was the question on many people's minds following the death of Justice Ruth Bader Ginsburg, with the Supreme Court on the verge of a conservative 6-3 majority. And now that President Trump's choice, Amy Coney Barrett, has been approved by the Senate, the Court is likely to have the votes to overturn the landmark 1973 decision that established Americans' right to terminate a pregnancy.

Some have imagined a future similar to Handmaid's Tale in which women are forced to carry children. Meanwhile, anti-abortion activists are covertly preparing a baby boom after all Americans are obliged to carry their pregnancies to term.

However, removing Roe will not end abortion in America. It will put an end to legal abortion in most of America.

This will have serious consequences for many people, particularly low-income Americans and people of color in red regions where the repeal of Roe would almost certainly close down the few remaining clinics. "This is already an abortion desert," the executive director of the Mississippi Reproductive Freedom Fund, Laurie Bertram Roberts, told Vox. "You're actually talking about an abortion wasteland" if Roe is repealed.

However, this does not mean that people who choose to terminate a pregnancy are completely powerless. Abortion charities around the country would continue their work, with some patients flying to blue states to obtain the procedure. Community-based providers that conduct abortions outside of the mainstream medical system are likely to remain in business. Self-managed abortion, in which patients perform their own abortions using medications, would also play a larger role.

Activists and clinicians will have to do a lot to prepare for that reality, from raising money to battling legislation that might send people to jail for self-managing abortions. Individuals in America have been terminating their pregnancies long before Roe v. Wade or even abortion clinics existed, and a judicial judgement will not stop them. It will only change the appearance of their alternatives — and the risks connected with them.

The history of abortion law in the United States is complicated.

It is helpful to understand the history of abortion in America in order to understand its future. Midwives provided the majority of reproductive health care in this country for many years, from labor and delivery through abortion. "The origin myth in the United States is that women dominated reproductive health care," writes Michele Bratcher Goodwin, a law professor at UC Irvine and author of the book Invisible Women and the Criminalization of Motherhood: Policing the Womb Outside the federal courthouse in Los Angeles, California, a "Rock for Abortion Rights" concert, rally, and march were held.

Before the end of slavery, half of midwives were Black, a quarter were Indigenous, and another quarter were white, according to Goodwin. They mostly cared for patients at home, and there were no restrictions prohibiting them from performing abortions prior to "quickening," or the point at which a pregnant woman may feel the fetus move (typically about 16 to 18 weeks) (usually around 16 to 18 weeks). That started to change in the mid-nineteenth century, when male doctors launched a drive to displace midwives and gain control of reproductive care.

These doctors began to fight for abortion restrictions through the American Medical Association, which was founded in 1847, in part to discourage midwives from performing the procedure. It is effective. According to Goodwin, by the beginning of the twentieth century, the percentage of reproductive care supplied by midwives had decreased. Abortion legislation spread across the country, with most states prohibiting the procedure by 1880.

In the decades afterwards, anybody seeking an abortion had to either locate a doctor who would perform the procedure illegally a quicker process for those with money or attempt to stop the pregnancy with medicines, turpentine, or, yes, coat hangers. Such surgeries may be dangerous, but the specific mortality toll is unknown because fatalities from covert abortions are rarely recorded. And, while abortion remained illegal, it became significantly safer in the mid-twentieth century with the increased use of antibiotics. Underground provider networks, like as the Jane collective, founded in Chicago in 1969, also arose to assist patients in obtaining abortions, collaborating with local doctors and even doing the procedure themselves.

Meanwhile, states like California were liberalizing their abortion laws in the 1960s. In rulings such as Griswold v. Connecticut, a 1965 decision that swept down state prohibitions on married couples' use of birth control, the Supreme Court was also laying the groundwork for constitutionally guaranteed reproductive rights. In 1973, the Court abolished all remaining state abortion prohibitions in one fell swoop, ruling in Roe v. Wade that governments could not impose an undue barrier on Americans' right to abortion.

Roe has subsequently curtailed what states may do to regulate abortion. Despite these constraints, they have accomplished a great deal. States in the South and Midwest passed a flurry of legislation limiting abortion clinic operations, including as requiring doctors to have admitting privileges at a local hospital, particularly after 2010, when Republicans took control of multiple state legislatures. As a result, hundreds of clinics in those areas closed, leaving many states with only a few if any options for patients seeking an abortion. Furthermore, restrictions requiring ultrasounds and waiting periods before a patient could have an abortion increased the expense of the procedure and made it more time consuming for patients. The Hyde Amendment, established in 1978, also prohibits Medicaid from financing most abortions, requiring low-income Americans to pay out of pocket even if they have the least means.

Many Americans now must travel hundreds of miles and pay hundreds, if not thousands, of dollars to have an abortion, if they can obtain one at all. And people of color, LGBTQ Americans, and illegal immigrants face disproportionately significant barriers to terminating a pregnancy. "Roe is and has never been enough to safeguard our communities," said Amanda Beatriz Williams, executive director of the Lilith Fund, a Texas abortion fund.

Years of restraints have forced supporters to adapt.

Because of the ongoing march of limitations in many jurisdictions, proponents of abortion rights have practiced aiding patients in obtaining the operation under difficult circumstances. In Mississippi, for example, where just one abortion facility remains open, the Mississippi Reproductive Freedom Fund provides financial assistance to approximately a dozen patients each week for abortion procedures or travel to a clinic. Many others benefit from the fund's practical assistance, such as locating the nearest clinic or determining how many pay periods they have left to save money for an abortion before it's too late. "We're like abortion concierges, but also like travel agents," Roberts explained.

Roberts isn't sure how many people the fund has assisted over the years, but others have - the New Orleans Abortion Fund, for example, has helped over 1,500 patients get abortions since it was founded in 2012.

Meanwhile, an increasing number of individuals are opting to perform their own abortions outside of the recognized medical system, typically with the drug misoprostol. A doctor can also administer the pill in conjunction with another prescription, mifepristone, and the regimen is approved by the Food and Drug Administration for use in abortions up to 10 weeks' gestation. However, due to the difficulties of traveling to a clinic to receive the drugs whether due to prejudice in medical settings or just wanting privacy in terminating their pregnancies some people purchase the medication online or through a friend or other source, and take it on their own.

It's difficult to say how many people go this route since self-managed abortions take place outside of established procedures for tracking patients and surgeries. However, experts believe that 1 to 4% of abortions are self-managed, according to Farah Diaz-Tello, senior attorney at the reproductive rights legal group If/When/How.

Despite these low numbers, there is evidence that abortion restrictions may increase interest in self-managed abortion - one recent study found that demand for abortion medications via an internet service were greater in areas with severe abortion regulations.

According to specialists, self-managed abortion can be a safe option for many people. In general, pharmacological abortion causes complications in less than 1% of cases. While getting the medication online or elsewhere outside the medical system means the pills haven't gone through the FDA's system for regulating medication content, a recent study of abortion pills ordered online by the reproductive research organization Gynuity found that most contained enough of the appropriate medication to be effective.

Finally, one of the primary risks of self-managed abortion is not the drug's bad effects, but the illegal repercussions of using it. Five states have laws directly prohibiting the practice, including Delaware, South Carolina, Arizona, Idaho, and Oklahoma, and many more have laws against "feticide" or other offenses that can be used to punish persons who self-manage. However, If/When/How and other organizations have been advocating for years to remove criminal penalties for self-managing abortion, and they have had some success for example, New York's Reproductive Health Act, which was passed in 2019, decriminalized self-managed abortion as part of a larger reform of the state's abortion law.

Another part of the abortion scene, as in previous decades, has been community-based abortion providers who perform the procedure outside of a medical institution. While some help people get and use abortion drugs, others, as Nina Liss-Schultz of Mother Jones writes, even perform surgical procedures such as vacuum aspiration. While their numbers are unknown because to the legal ambiguity of their profession, one such provider told Mother Jones that she knows up to 75 individuals who perform at-home abortions or educate others.

Providing abortions outside of the medical system is far more legally risky than receiving them, as most abortion laws in the United States target providers rather than patients. However, If/When/How and other organizations have been advocating for their rights, as well as the rights of those seeking abortions. "May not be enough for the law simply not to penalize people who abort their own pregnancies," Diaz-Tello went on. "We must make certain that criminalization does not destroy communities and that people are not removed from community-based care systems that keep them safe." While activists and providers have already organized in response to abortion restrictions, the collapse of Roe would need a new level of engagement.

According to the Guttmacher Institute, twenty-one states have legislation on the books that might be used to criminalize abortion if the ruling is overturned. This includes ten states, such as Louisiana and Mississippi, that have "trigger prohibitions" in place to restrict abortion immediately if Roe is overturned. In such places, reversing Roe would almost probably have an immediate impact on clinics.

"It's almost as if someone walked along one day and clicked their fingers and all legal abortion access vanished," Roberts said.

But that doesn't mean abortion would stop.

If/When/How, for example, will continue to strive to legalize self-managed abortion as it has in the past. "We're concerned about the future of abortion rights jurisprudence," Diaz-Tello said, "but nothing changes for us because, in many ways, Roe isn't relevant to the question of whether people should avoid jail time for terminating their own pregnancies."

And, they conclude, the effort done by abortion charities and others in recent years may have helped prepare them for the repeal of Roe. For example, the Covid-19 epidemic drove numerous groups to work even harder, while legislators in states like as Texas campaigned to outlaw abortions, claiming that they were unnecessary medical procedures.

"We had a taste of a post-Roe state when Texas's Governor Abbott utilized the Covid-19 epidemic to shut down abortion facilities in Texas," said Williams, executive director of the Lilith Fund. "We joined forces to strategize, construct communication lines, provide real-time information, and manage logistics," the group stated.

"We'd continue to expand our regional relationships, and we'd continue to build out our infrastructure so that we can do whatever it takes to ensure individuals get the care they need," Williams said if Roe were overturned.

Many grassroots organizations will face difficult challenges in the coming months. For one reason, advocates believe that self-managed abortion cannot and should not be the exclusive choice for patients, especially while legal sanctions remain in place in so many locations. "SMA will not replace clinics," Roberts emphasized.

The repeal of Roe will almost surely result in an influx of individuals from red states wanting to travel to blue states for treatment, similar to what happened during the pandemic, when clinics in Colorado, New Mexico, and Nevada had a 706 percent increase in patients arriving from Texas. However, in a post-Roe future, it would not only be Texas; while it is unclear how other state legislatures would react, states with trigger bans alone would create large "abortion wastelands," as Roberts puts it. Patients in Arkansas, Louisiana, Mississippi, Tennessee, and Kentucky, for example, may find themselves without a clinic in their state.

They might wish to go to Illinois, where providers and campaigners have already campaigned to boost service in anticipation of future constraints. Even if physicians in those and other liberal states can manage the influx, patients would need money to travel - a big hurdle because abortion funds in areas with the most need and fewest resources also have the least cash on hand, according to Roberts.

"I honestly don't know of any Southern fund or clinic that can genuinely declare we're completely prepared for a post-Roe existence," Roberts said. "None of us have enough money."

She highlighted that they will need money not just to pay patients in the months following Roe, but also to fight for access in the years to follow: "We'll need money to organize in order to change state legislation."

Unless and until those rules are amended, the future of abortion without Roe might be a return to a time when women conducted the operation at home or in their communities but without the laissez-faire legal framework that permitted them to do so without fear. Abortion treatment is "being reintroduced to women but under the fear of criminal penalty," according to Goodwin, with the rise of self-managed abortion and community-based providers.

For many, the challenge now, and in any post-Roe future, is how to remove that shadow and how to ensure that the many people who still want abortions at clinics may have them. It's a difficult battle, but many claim they've got plenty of practice fighting it.

What Americans Think About Abortion

The Occasionally Surprising Poll Results As the Supreme Court reverses Roe v. Wade,

While the Supreme Court overturned Roe v. Wade, allowing states to outlaw abortion, a review of national polls shows that many Americans are consistently split between identifying as "pro-choice" or "pro-life," a clear majority supports keeping the process is legitimate support varies depending on the circumstances.

Abortion rights have widespread support: Gallup polls show that in May 2021, Americans support abortion in all or most cases at 80 percent, only slightly higher than in 1975 (76 percent), and the Pew Research Center finds that 59 percent of adults believe abortion should be legal, up from 60 percent in 1995—though there has been fluctuation, with support dropping to 47 percent in 2009.

In a Gallup poll, the number of Americans who feel abortion is morally acceptable hit a record high of 47 percent in May, up from a low of 36 percent in 2009, while a Quinnipiac poll indicated support for abortion being legal in all or most situations reached a near-record high of 63 percent in September.

Support for Roe v. Wade has been consistent, with a November Quinnipiac survey indicating that 63 percent agree with the court's verdict, and 72 percent of respondents in a January Marquette Law School poll and 69 percent of January CNN poll respondents opposing it being reversed.

A January CNN poll found that 59 percent of people want their state to have abortion laws that are "more permissive than restrictive" if Roe is overturned, while only 20 percent want their state to outright ban abortion (another 20 percent want it to be restricted but not outright banned) (another 20 percent want it to be restricted but not banned).

strongest pro-abortion sentiment—within limits According to a June Associated Press/NORC poll, 87 percent favor abortion when the woman's life is in danger, 84 percent support exceptions in cases of rape or incest, and 74 percent support abortion if the child is born with a life-threatening condition.

As the pregnancy progresses, according to the AP/NORC poll, 61 percent believe abortion should be legal in the first trimester, but only 34 percent in the second and 19 percent in the third, and an April Wall Street Journal poll found that more Americans approve of 15-week abortion bans than disapprove.

Partisan divide—but not in all cases: Democrats are statistically far more likely to support abortion rights than Republicans, with Quinnipiac finding in September that only 39 percent of Republicans believe abortion should be legal in all or most cases versus 89 percent of Democrats—though exceptions for rape and incest and when the mother's life is at risk are supported by 70 percent and 76 percent of Republicans, respectively.

Americans with religious affiliations are far more likely to oppose abortion than the nonreligious (82 percent believe abortion should be legal), but with the exception of white evangelical Protestants (77 percent believe abortion should be illegal), a higher share of every religious group polled—white non-evangelicals, black Protestants, and Catholics—favor abortion rights.

Gender disparities are not as great as you would think. Women are somewhat more likely than men to support abortion, with Pew indicating that 62 percent of women want abortion to be legalized, compared to 56 percent of men.

According to Pew Research, majorities of all races support abortion legalization, but support was higher among black (67 percent believe it should be legal) and Asian (68 percent) respondents than white and Hispanic (57 percent and 58 percent, respectively) respondents (57 percent and 58 percent , respectively).

The Pew poll indicated that support for abortion is highest among those aged 18-29 (67 percent feel it should be legal), followed by 61 percent of those aged 30-49, 53 percent of those aged 50-64, and 55 percent of those aged 65 and up.

Support grows with education. Pew reported that 68 percent of college graduates support legalization, compared to 61 percent of those with some college and 50 percent with a high school diploma or less (a Washington Post/ABC survey found a similar pattern).

Parents are less likely to support abortion rights. According to All In Together's September poll with Lake

Research and Emerson College Polling, 36 percent of those with children opposed the Texas near-total abortion ban versus 54.9 percent of those without children, and the Post/ABC poll found 58 percent of parents want the Supreme Court to uphold Roe v. Wade versus 62 percent of non-parents.

According to the Post/ABC, 71 percent of those in the Northeast want Roe v. Wade to be upheld, compared to 58 percent in the Midwest, 53 percent in the South, and 66 percent in the West, and urban residents are more likely to support Roe v. Wade (with 69 percent of support) than those in suburban or rural areas (56 percent and 57 percent, respectively).

The Post/ABC poll found that 59 percent of those earning less than $50,000 per year wanted the court to keep the legislation, compared to 62 percent of those earning $50,000-$100,000 and 65 percent of those earning more than $100,000.

The Biden administration is expanding access to the monkeypox vaccine in states with high case rates.

Impressive Fact

While public opinion on whether abortion should be legalized has been mostly stable since 1995, the number of Americans who identify as "pro-choice" or "pro-life" has not. According to Gallup, 49 percent of Americans currently identify as pro-choice and 47 percent as pro-life, compared to 56 percent and 33 percent in 1995, respectively. Though a majority of Americans have always supported abortion being legal in some circumstances, in 2019, 2013, 2012, 2010, and 2009, more respondents identified as pro-life than pro-choice.

The American Tangent

According to a May 2021 Ipsos survey, Americans' support for abortion lags well below that of many other nations, with 66 percent believing abortion should be legal in certain situations, compared to a worldwide average of 71 percent. Sweden has the highest rate of abortion support (88 percent), followed by the Netherlands (85 percent) and France (81 percent), whereas Brazil, India, South Africa, Colombia, Mexico, Turkey, Peru, and Malaysia have lower rates of abortion support than the United States.

Important background

The Supreme Court's 1973 Roe v. Wade decision, which affirmed the constitutional right to an abortion, made abortion lawful statewide for the first time. The court subsequently upheld that decision in Whole Woman's Health v. Hellerstedt in 2016, declaring that states cannot establish abortion restrictions that create an "undue hardship" on the procedure. Republican state legislators have repeatedly targeted abortion in an attempt to persuade the Supreme Court to reconsider its precedent. However, according to the pro-abortion rights Guttmacher Institute, states have imposed more than 1,300 abortion restrictions since Roe v. Wade was decided in 1973, with over 100 cases decided this year alone. Abortion opponents scored a number of victories in 2021, when the conservative-leaning Supreme Court decided to hear a challenge to Mississippi's abortion law and revisit Roe v. Wade. Texas subsequently implemented the most stringent abortion restrictions in the United States since Roe v. Wade when Senate Bill 8 (SB 8) went into effect on September 1, prohibiting practically all abortions after six weeks, which Idaho and Oklahoma have already emulated.

Chapter Five

PRO-CHOICE IS A HUMAN RIGHT.

America is about to find out just how pro-life Republicans are. Following the Roe decision, some abortion opponents believe it is time to focus on strengthening America's social safety net. Will the rest of their movement follow suit?

Paying pregnant women's bills was not part of Nathan and Emily Berning's life plan—until they discovered that doing so significantly reduced the number of women seeking abortions. Atoria Foley, who was living in her truck when she discovered she was pregnant, was among the first. Atoria had scheduled an abortion, and the Bernings jumped into action. They flew her to Sacramento, California, and put her up at a hotel. They covered what Atoria needed, such as groceries, petrol, and vehicle payments, sometimes with their own money. They registered her for every government benefit they could find. The Bernings were relieved when Atoria canceled her abortion appointment. Kiahari, her kid, turned two in March.

Three years have passed since the Indiana couple founded Let Them Live, a company that provides financial assistance to women in order to deter them from having abortions. The group has paid $2.4 million in expenses for pregnant women, and the Bernings think they have prevented over 400 abortions. (Let Them Live asks these women to promise to forgo having abortions in exchange for financial assistance.) Nathan informed me that the Bernings have never actually advocated for the repeal of Roe v. Wade. But now that the judgement has been reversed, Nathan hopes that the anti-abortion movement will shift its focus to advocating for public policies that benefit women and families. Nonprofits like his "can contribute a percentage of the answer to the problem," he adds, but there must be a government side to it. Generally speaking, the pro-life movement has not thought big enough. "

Members of this movement have fought for decades to get to this stage. They only need to determine what to do next. Nathan Berning is one of many abortion opponents who would want to see the social safety net expanded significantly. I spoke with a dozen others who felt that advocating for things like universal child care and a higher minimum wage was the obvious next step for the movement. But theirs is a minority voice in the wider anti-abortion group. For decades, most abortion opponents have been allied with a party that has fought vehemently against government expansion. That collaboration is likely to stymie any progress toward better results for women and families.

Members of the anti-abortion movement are cognizant of the reality that abortion will be difficult—if not impossible—to get in many parts of the country. According to a recent 10-year study, most people who seek abortions express financial concerns, and women who are denied access to abortion are more likely to be poor even years later. "There will probably be more unexpected childbirths now that Roe is gone, and that's going to have an effect on expanding the breadth of poverty in the United States", explained Mark Rank, a social scientist and professor at Washington University in St. Louis.

Almost every member of the anti-abortion movement believes that pregnant women and families should be supported through private means such as charities and churches. Where they most disagree is on the role of government. " Kori Porter, CEO of Christian Solidarity

Worldwide USA, told me in an email that activists should be prepared for an increase in demand for domestic-abuse centers, foster homes, and childcare relief. She added that the same energy that inspired many to stand for hours on sweltering sidewalks with placards, make numerous calls to their congressman, march, and selflessly contribute endless dollars must be the same force exhorted to now demand early education, food assistance, and childcare relief. Charlie Camosy, a Creighton University School of Medicine ethics professor and Religion News Service anti-abortion writer, has long advocated for paid family leave, a higher minimum wage, and Medicaid expansion. The 26 states that will soon have the strictest abortion restrictions also have the lowest average minimum incomes. (Medicaid has not yet been expanded in ten states.) Conservative pro-lifers need to adopt a diversified strategy, according to Camosy. "They've made hardly any progress on policy."

Camosy has benefited from recent private and governmental initiatives, particularly on the Catholic left. Last month, the United States Conference of Catholic Bishops urged lawmakers to extend the increased child tax credit in order to tackle child poverty. Dioceses in California, Maryland, and Washington State have launched projects to give free baby products and health services to expectant mothers. In anticipation of Roe v. Wade, Notre Dame's de Nicola Center for Ethics and Culture launched a new social-science effort to research optimal strategies for reducing poverty that its leaders believe would influence public policy. Senator Mitt Romney of Utah recently introduced a new version of his child-tax-credit proposal, which a number of anti-abortion groups have already signed on to, and Senator Marco Rubio just issued a list of efforts to assist pregnant women and families. A few Republican states have also expanded Medicaid coverage to include postpartum mothers.

People in Camosy's camp are optimistic that the repeal of Roe would free anti-abortion Americans from the limits of their political party and empower them to campaign for pro-family legislation. They argue that failing to do so would be hypocritical. Some anti-abortion Republicans may be prepared to bend on government spending, especially after Donald Trump steered the GOP in a far more populist direction; Roe's reversal may hasten the conversation. "There is now an extremely important opportunity for pro-life Republicans to be more vociferous in their support for social-welfare programs," Camosy noted.

If everything appears a little too rosy, it probably is. As the GOP adage goes, "the government that governs best governs the least." The communities in America with the strictest abortion restrictions are also places where people are skeptical of government interference, and spending millions more on government services is a political nonstarter.

The most renowned and influential anti-abortion activists are likely to focus only on reducing the number of abortions, rather than lobbying for greater social spending to help women who cannot have them. They'll concentrate on increasing abortion restrictions in red states and enacting whatever restrictions they can in blue and purple states. Expanding the federal government's social safety net is "a matter for later," according to Mallory Carroll, vice president of communications for Susan B. Anthony Pro-Life America. Due to gestational limits, we are now preserving infants and bolstering the social support that already exists.

These organizations will continue to seek assistance for women and families in the same way they have in the past: through charities and individual donations. In preparation for a world without Roe, the SBA established a network of services for pregnant women, mostly funded by churches and other religious organizations. This approach is based on a decades-old strategy: Since Roe v. Wade in 1973, abortion opponents have invested millions of dollars in pregnancy-resource centers that assist pregnant women with counseling and supplies; a few of these groups now provide free medical treatment. When Texas made abortion illegal after six weeks last year, the state government transferred $100 million to these institutions. Mississippi Republicans adopted a bill that will provide $3.5 million in tax breaks to pregnancy assistance centers.

One issue with such endeavors is that they are little balls. Certain aspects of what they provide are beneficial to some pregnant women in the short term. (Abortion-rights supporters contend that the more basic issue is that women who desire abortions are unable to obtain them.) However, they are insufficient to alleviate the magnitude of economic stress on families. "If you truly want to close the gap in poverty, you need to take action at the federal and state levels," said Rank, a social scientist. According to Rank, Romney's Family Security Act idea has promise, but many progressives oppose it since it is based on job requirements and would exclude the country's poorest families.

The Supreme Court's decision to overturn Roe v. Wade changed the face of American politics this week. Even in this new landscape, Americans can presumably expect much more of the same: a growing divide between blue and red states. According to Mary Ziegler, a regular Atlantic writer and law professor at Florida State University, anti-abortion groups are far more likely to lobby for – and gain – enhanced government assistance for pregnant women and families than any other group. She added that in Republican-dominated states, "the focus has been and will continue to be on punishing the person supplying the abortion—not supporting the individual seeking the abortion."

Anti-abortion campaigners are likely to pursue challenges against interstate abortion travel as well as prohibitions on the abortion medication mifepristone. Some of the most ardent supporters are already working on legislation to punish women who have them. The Texas-based organization Foundation to Abolish Abortion assisted in the creation of a Louisiana bill that would allow manslaughter charges against women who terminate their pregnancies.

Abortion opponents who oppose a social safety net may come to believe that boosting social spending is the best way to reduce abortions. According to research, restricting access to abortion does not reduce demand. "I think that after a few years, [when] they discover that these legislation didn't have the substantial impact that they had hoped for," Daniel K. Williams, a history professor at the University of West Georgia, told me. In other words, Roe's death is unlikely to be the catalyst that propels the movement forward. If that day comes, it will be later in life.

Nathan Berning was a rather conservative man until he and his wife founded Let Them Live. He'd worked for Ben Carson's presidential campaign in 2016. He wasn't a supporter of the government interfering in people's private lives or bailing out families with public funds. His perspective has evolved in the last three years. "I've seen what these mothers go through personally," he explained.

Berning put me in touch with Atoria, who is now 26 and lives in Sacramento with Kiahari in her own apartment. (She was attempting to stop him from putting grapes in their waffle maker while we were on the phone.) She doesn't necessarily see the end of Roe as a cause for celebration. She sees it as a chance for the movement that drove her to continue with her pregnancy to show their support. She explained that there must now be a domino effect of [more] government assistance and programs to empower women. Without it, overturning Roe "makes no sense."

Abortion rights haven't

Anticipating a society in which abortion is no longer a fundamental right and spurred on by a draft Supreme Court opinion that foreshadows this seismic shift, blue states are strengthening their reproductive-rights legislation. The effort is not only to defend reproductive freedom and care for women and girls who live in their states, but also to provide a "safe haven" for those who live in jurisdictions where abortion is likely to be illegal.

Months back, the Connecticut legislature passed legislation to protect doctors and patients from lawsuits brought by states where abortion is illegal. Oregon lawmakers granted $15 million in March for expanded abortion access, in part to deal with an influx of patients from neighboring Idaho, which has imposed a six-week abortion limit. In California, around a dozen reproductive-rights bills are making their way through the legislature, while the governor and legislators are pushing to include such rights in the state constitution.

There is a widespread understanding that abortion rights are being challenged across most of the nation, according to Elizabeth Nash, who monitors state laws for the Guttmacher Institute, which does research and promotes reproductive rights.

Both sides of the abortion debate agree that the Roe v. Wade decision was only "the beginning." As California and others work to create safe havens for reproductive rights, the states may find themselves in legal conflict with one another.

If the Supreme Court overturns the landmark 1973 abortion-rights decision in Roe v. Wade, abortion access in the United States will be severely harmed. That appears to be the court's direction, as revealed by a draft majority ruling leaked to Politico this week with explosive political and cultural impact. With that, decades of battles in and between states will form their own policies, right up to the top court.

According to Guttmacher, in a post-Roe world, 26 states are guaranteed or likely to restrict abortion - throughout the South, the middle of the country, and the West. These states either have pre-Roe laws on the books or in their constitutions, have "trigger" laws that go into effect if Roe is overturned, or have previously implemented severely restrictive legislation, such as eliminating exemptions for rape or incest and making abortion a criminal. Women in such states have three choices: carry on with undesired pregnancies, self-induce abortions using medicine or risky methods, or fly to sanctuary states.

"Access to medication abortion is critical," says Ms. Nash, and it accounts for more than half of all abortions in the United States today. Travel is both costly and exhausting. She points out that for someone in Louisiana looking for abortion access, the next state would be Illinois, a 1,300-mile round trip. Because three-quarters of abortion patients earn low wages and the majority are already parents, many would be unable to arrange for child care or afford to take time off work or travel to a distant location.

And travel continues to take place. Patients from Texas, which enacted a six-week ban last year (before many women realize they are pregnant), are traveling as far as Washington and Maryland, with an estimated 1,400 traveling each month since the restriction went into effect in September. Wait times at nearby clinics in Colorado and Illinois can range from three to four weeks.

Roe v. Wade shockwaves across America.

"Capacity will be stretched very thin in states that retain access," Ms. Nash adds. "You're simply witnessing a massive breakdown in access to care." You can see why progressive states are strengthening abortion rights."

California will create a "template" for blue states.

California has always been a leader in reproductive rights. Gov. Gavin Newsom signed legislation in March that makes abortion more accessible by eliminating copays and deductibles from commercial health insurance and the state's low-income Medicaid plan. The insurance policies must cover the entire cost. He sees recommendations from a newly formed advisory board, as well as the ensuing slate of laws currently passing through the legislature, as a "template" for other states, portraying California as a "beacon of hope."

Abortion is available in more than 160 clinics in this deep blue state, but abortion activists argue that this is insufficient. There are no such clinics in 40% of counties, and California is also dealing with an influx of patients from other states. The policies would help to close these gaps by increasing capacity, such as by funding more training for health care professionals and allowing nurse practitioners with adequate training to perform first-trimester abortions. Grants would also be given to organizations that help low-income patients, including those from out of state, as well as professionals who are not compensated for their work with low-income patients.

Another set of regulations would shield patients and providers from civil liability judgments based on laws in other jurisdictions, as well as strengthen privacy safeguards for abortion-related medical data from enforcement by law enforcement and outside parties of abortion restrictions in other states. Connecticut's recently enacted legislation would prohibit the governor from extraditing someone to another state if what they did in Connecticut was legal. Colorado's governor signed legislation in April explicitly protecting abortion rights and prohibiting public institutions from rejecting such rights. As of March, a Washington legislation prohibits the state from pursuing legal action against abortion seekers and those who assist them.

"UNRESOLVED LAW"

This type of legislation is a reaction to any Texas-style limitation that allows private individuals to sue anybody accused of assisting with an abortion. Abortion supporters are particularly concerned about a Missouri-style measure that would make it illegal for a person to go out of state to have an abortion. That attempt in Missouri failed.

According to Cary Franklin, a professor at the University of California, Los Angeles School of Law and an expert on reproductive rights and gender issues, such cross-border processes would create a new front on the abortion battlefield. She highlighted interstate abortion litigation as "unsettled law" that might lead to several court battles.

"The irony is that [the Supreme Legal's] decision is going to spark so much more discussion, disagreement, and legal fights," she says. "The states will now be at odds with one another."

She and others believe that the best way to protect abortion rights in a state is to include them in the state constitution. Although 16 states and Washington, D.C. have made reproduction rights legal, Guttmacher believes that future legislatures may easily change such legislation. Constitutions are extremely tough to change.

That is why, despite having a right to privacy in the state constitution that protects abortion, Democratic leaders in California are now seeking special constitutional protection. The huge Democratic majority in the legislature suggests that they might secure the two-thirds majority required to amend the constitution, putting the idea before voters in November. According to surveys last year, 79 percent of potential voters do not want Roe v. Wade overturned.

"California will codify this right in our state constitution because we know we cannot rely on the Supreme Court to defend reproductive rights," the statement reads. The governor declared, "Women will be safeguarded here." and legislative leaders said in a joint statement on May 2. Vermont voters will also have the opportunity to vote on a constitutional amendment protecting abortion rights in November.

Professor Franklin believes that even this might be vulnerable to a Supreme Court decision. If the Supreme Court rules on fetal personhood, indicating that a fetus has a constitutional right to life, as the anti-abortion camp asserts, it would overrule state constitutions, she says, but it would depend on the terminology. "Fetal personhood is without a doubt the end," she continues.

Chapter Six

<u>A   NEW   PHASE'S "BEGINNING"</u>

Abortion supporters and opponents see a Roe v. Wade decision as the "beginning" of a new era in America's deeply divisive and important debate.

The pro-life movement is just getting started, according to Jonathan Keller, head of the anti-abortion organization California Family Council. The battle will transfer from the courts to the statehouse, where state elections will "matter more than ever" as legislators decide on reproductive policy.

He believes that people who oppose abortion rights should support candidates that provide "real-world services to women and families confronting unwanted pregnancies." This includes more funding for family resource centers, paid family leave, and enhanced maternity care. "It will provide us a fantastic opportunity to put our money where our mouth is."

A THIRD OPINION ON ABORTION

Why do we need a third abortion option in Europe?

I've been immersed in the following tidal flow of news items, opinion articles, blogs, and podcasts since learning about Samuel Alito's leaked draft ruling overturning Roe v. Wade. The New York Times podcast The Daily is one of the few that provides balanced coverage. They dedicated two pieces to the Alito draft, the first to passionate anti-abortion campaigner comments, and the second to abortion providers.

It's hardly surprise that The Daily only listened to individuals working on the outside of this sensitive subject; that's how abortion is typically covered in America. Who wants to hear people who haven't given it much consideration ramble on about their contradictory emotions?

And, as a May 6 Pew Research report shows, the American people are highly confused about abortion. Sixty-one percent of respondents say abortion should be legal in some or all circumstances, while 37 percent believe it should be illegal in all or most cases.

That appears to be a decisive victory for the pro-choice side, but it isn't. Only 19% of respondents believe abortion should be legal in all circumstances. However, there is certainly no agreement on the pro-life alternative. Only 8% of Americans believe abortion should be prohibited in all circumstances.

According to the majority of Americans, resistance to abortion increases dramatically after the first trimester of pregnancy. Most Americans believe that the stage of the pregnancy matters, with opposition to abortion skyrocketing after the first trimester. Fifty-eight percent of respondents disagreed with the statement, "The decision to have an abortion should be entirely up to the pregnant woman."

The pro-life slogan "human life begins at conception, hence a fetus is a person with rights" was rejected by 65 percent of respondents. Seventy-one percent of Americans fall somewhere in the middle of the debate, believing that the practice should be either "largely legal" or "mainly criminal."

While 47% of Americans believe abortion is ethically wrong in most or all situations, only 22% believe it should always, or nearly always, be illegal.

Opinions that are passionate

The Daily reached out to abortion doctors and pro-life activists because they routinely express unambiguous, unapologetic, and passionate views.

Susan Dodd, an abortionist from Knoxville, Tenn., became upset as she reflected on the women she served at her clinic.

"So many of them had such tragic stories about—this is why I'm doing it," she said. "And, you know, I have three children at home, my husband and I both work full-time, and our birth control has failed." "I can scarcely feed the three I have," she lamented, her voice quivering. "You may simply read story after story after story."

The pro-life proponents interviewed by The Daily live in a separate moral realm. Ohio Right to Life President Michael Gonidakis didn't want people to think he didn't care about pregnant women: "It's incumbent upon us now to work even harder to ensure that we have social services and a safety net for women who find themselves burdened with a pregnancy."

But his main goal outweighed his concerns. He contended that getting rid of Roe was merely the beginning. The next goal is to pass legislation to keep anti-abortion drugs out of the hands of women and to prevent these women from accessing abortion providers in neighboring states.

"The number of women flying to Kansas has actually increased significantly," Gonidakis remarked. "And the number of people flying to Illinois has absolutely skyrocketed." So that's the problem we're up against. And how do you create legislation to address that? "

American Republikans' ideas have not changed.

The reporter conducting these interviews, Sabrina Tavernise, never asked pro-life people to respond to pro-choice arguments, and vice versa. Both sides were able to express themselves freely. This is also unsurprising. Only 36% of Americans say they have given the abortion issue serious thought.

And it's obvious. Many people feel that life starts at conception, while others believe that the decision should be left completely to the pregnant woman. These people are, to use a popular expression, "cross-pressured."

Most Americans' attitudes against abortion haven't changed much in decades. Support for the legality of abortion in most or all situations has increased by one percentage point (61 percent) since 1990, while support for the procedure's illegality in all or most cases has decreased by one percentage point during the same period.

As everyone is aware, public opinion on abortion is sharply divided along political and religious lines. However, according to the Pew poll, just 13% of Republicans believe abortion should be illegal in all circumstances, and 64% believe pregnancy stage matters.

In contrast, only 30% of Democrats believe abortion should be legalized without restrictions.

The stark disparity is that 47 percent of Republicans believe abortion should be "largely prohibited," while only 15 percent of Democrats agree.

73% of white evangelicals say their religion influences their abortion views, compared to 41% of Catholics and only 28% of white non-evangelical Protestants. On the other hand, just 21% of white evangelicals believe abortion should be illegal in all instances, while about one-quarter believe it should be legal in all or most cases.

In contrast, 60% of non-evangelical white Protestants, 66% of black Protestants, and 56% of Catholics believe abortion should be legal in all or most cases. Nonetheless, 53% of white evangelicals agree with the statement, "There are certain circumstances when abortion should be authorized, and others where it should not be permitted."

Even if American men remained mute on the matter of abortion (as some women believe they should), the Pew survey findings would be minimally impacted.

The big difference is that 47 percent of Republicans believe abortion should be "mostly illegal," while only 15 percent of Democrats believe the same.

73% of white evangelicals say their religion influences their views on abortion, compared to 41% of Catholics and 28% of white non-evangelical Protestants. On the other hand, only 21% of white evangelicals believe abortion should be illegal in all circumstances, while nearly a quarter believe it should be legal in all or most cases.

Abortion should be lawful in all or most instances, according to 60% of non-evangelical white Protestants, 66% of black Protestants, and 56% of Catholics. Nonetheless, 53% of white evangelicals agree with the statement, "There are some situations in which abortion should be legal, and others in which it should not be legal."

Even if American men stopped talking about abortion (as some women believe they should), the Pew survey results would be unaffected.

Even if American men stopped talking about abortion (as some women believe they should), the Pew survey results would be unaffected. In most cases, 42 percent of women and 41 percent of men believe abortion should be legal. In contrast, only 9% of women and 8% of men support a strong pro-life stance.

In general, anti-abortion sentiment grows with age. Seventy-four percent of those aged 18 to 29 believe abortion should be legal in all or most cases, compared to just 54 percent of those aged 65 and up.

Regional variations are also significant. Only 33% of Southerners believe abortion should be "generally available," while 34% of Midwesterners, 43% of Westerners, and 48% of Northeasterners agree.

Nonetheless, only 25% of Southerners and Midwesterners support an outright abortion ban.

Why are we yelling at each other?

So, if the American public is complex, why has the American debate devolved into a shouting match between supporters of opposing viewpoints? Furthermore, given that three-quarters of the population rejects strong pro-life and pro-choice orthodoxy, why has moderate opinion been excluded from the national debate?

The issue is partially sociological. If you are a white evangelical who is involved in Republican politics, you must be pro-life. Alternatively, if you teach at a secular university and associate with Democrats, you are either pro-choice or a closed-mouthed liberal. Nuance is not permitted in either social setting.

When the term "pro-life" is mentioned in a liberal setting, the air quickly fills with groans and complaints. When the pro-choice option is brought up in a conservative setting, the vitriol is deafening.

According to the Pew Research Center, many people, both liberal and conservative, are biting their tongues and covering their buttocks.

We must be clear about the Supreme Court's Roe v. Wade decision. According to the Roe decision, the state cannot regulate abortion during the first trimester of pregnancy. "The state may impose abortion regulations reasonably related to maternal health" in the second trimester. The fetus is determined to be "viable" in the third trimester, and the state is free to regulate, or even prohibit, abortion.

In contrast, abortion is legal in most of Europe during the first semester. After that, the procedure is prohibited, unless the woman's health is jeopardized. The European model is obviously too permissive for pro-life activists and too restrictive for pro-choice advocates, but it appears to be very close to the American middle.

One observer says the European model is too permissive for pro-life activists and too restrictive for pro-choice advocates, but it appears to be closely aligned with the American middle class, "According to one observer."

When the abortion debate devolves into a death match between supporters of the most extreme options, bad things happen. First and foremost, we demonize one another. Then, because the other side is demonic, no compromise is possible. So we go from Roe v. Wade (which gave the pro-choice faction a decisive victory) to a post-Roe world where pro-life views triumph.

If you live in a relatively liberal state, the repeal of Roe may not make much of a difference. Until conservative politicians enact a nationwide ban Otherwise, we will most likely find ourselves in a divided nation. Politicians in red states will sleep at night thinking of new ways to keep desperate women from fleeing to pro-choice America (if they can afford the cost of travel).

Three-quarters of Americans sympathize with both pro-choice and pro-life arguments. They do not believe that life begins at conception, but, like most Europeans, they believe that abortion should be limited to the first trimester unless the woman's health is jeopardized.

What if we started advocating for a third option? Let us refer to it as "the European option." We'd get slammed from both sides. That's fine. Except in exceptional circumstances, we'd make it.

But here's the deal: There can be no resolution, consensus, or peace as long as an unrepresentative 25%

of Americans continue to wage war on one another while the rest of us watch helplessly.

The time for silence has passed. If your abortion stance does not fit on a bumper sticker, simply ask, Access to safe abortion is restricted in countries other than Mexico. Even in the United States, where abortion is legal, services are difficult to come by. In fact, because of burdensome regulations, a lack of providers, insufficient funding, or political opposition, many women and girls face significant legal or financial barriers to accessing safe abortion services.

Obstacles to safe abortion appear to be on the rise in the United States. Since the landmark Roe v. Wade decision in 1973, which established women's right to choose abortion as a matter of privacy, both state and federal legislators have limited access to legal abortion. These rollback measures aim to accomplish one of two things:

restrict women's access to legal abortion (for example, through mandatory waiting periods or mandatory—and often manifestly inaccurate—counseling); or limit legal abortion access to specific populations (such as rape victims or ladies whose pregnancies imperil their lives).

Women with limited economic resources face additional barriers to safe abortion, resulting in discrimination against already marginalized women. Since 1977, federal funding for abortion services has been frozen, except in cases of life endangerment, rape, or incest. Furthermore, the majority of states do not fund abortion services that do not fall under these exceptions. A safe abortion can cost between $500 and $1,500. As a result, women with limited resources—who have not been raped or whose lives are not jeopardized by their pregnancy—may be forced to choose between carrying an unwanted pregnancy to term or resorting to desperate measures that could endanger their health.

Abortion Regulatory Barriers in the United States

The United States Supreme Court has consistently ruled that an outright ban on abortion is unconstitutional since 1973. The Court has, however, allowed states to regulate and limit abortion access as long as they do not impose an "undue" burden on the woman seeking to terminate her pregnancy.

Over the last decade, state and federal legislators have pushed the limits of this Supreme Court mandate, imposing regulations with the explicit goal of challenging the constitutionality of legal abortion. Many states enact regulations that, in practice, may be excessively burdensome. Some states, for example, require women and girls who want to terminate a pregnancy to seek counseling, which, in addition to being unsolicited, is frequently manifestly biased and medically unsound.

Incorrect or fabricated data

According to the nongovernmental research organization Alan Guttmacher Institute (AGI), as of September 2006, well over half of the states in the United States (32) required mandatory counseling for all women seeking abortion. Three states require clinics to inform women about a rumored link between abortion and breast cancer, which has been conclusively debunked by numerous scientific studies. Four other states also require women to be informed that the fetus may be capable of feeling pain at any point during the pregnancy. This information, however, contradicts recent scientific findings that fetuses cannot feel pain until the 29th week of gestation. Indeed, given that 90% of abortions in the United States occur within the first twelve weeks of pregnancy, the mandatory information on fetal pain is not only scientifically incorrect but also irrelevant to the vast majority of abortion patients.

Access to accurate and complete information on medical procedures is an essential component of the human right to the best health possible as well as the principle of informed consent. When health professionals are required to provide one-sided or inaccurate information about medical procedures to women and girls, as the law requires in many jurisdictions in the United States, the human right to health is jeopardized.

Waiting periods that are required cost money.

According to AGI, 24 of the 32 states that require mandatory counseling also require women and girls to wait a certain amount of time—usually 24 hours— between the counseling session and the abortion. While a waiting period before a medical procedure is not incompatible with the right to health in and of itself, it can create additional, and potentially unduly burdensome, barriers to access to safe and legal abortions. For example, in states where the law requires in-person counseling (rather than over the phone), a mandatory waiting period requires the patient to travel to the abortion facility at least twice. As a result, many people must miss work for several days, and where there are no abortion facilities nearby—and 87 percent of U.S. counties lack such facilities, according to the most recent data available—the mandatory waiting period may necessitate an overnight stay or several long-distance trips.

Girls Will Face New Restrictions

Many non-governmental organizations (NGOs) based in the United States observe that girls face more restrictions than adult women when it comes to access to safe abortion. According to AGI and NARAL Pro-Choice America, 44 states have laws in place requiring parental consent or notification prior to an abortion of a minor. More than 20 states have parental consent laws that require consent from a parent before a minor can obtain a legal abortion; in three cases, both parents must consent. Furthermore, more than ten states have laws requiring a parent to be notified of a minor's intention to have an abortion, and two states require both parents to be notified.

Mandatory parental consent and notification laws are problematic for a variety of reasons, particularly when both parents are required to consent or be notified.

According to abortion providers in the United States, the vast majority of teenage girls already seek support and guidance from one or both parents. The impact of notification and consent laws thus falls disproportionately on particularly vulnerable girls who are unable to involve their parents in their decision-making, including girls who have no contact with either or both parents.

International human rights law requires governments to prioritize the best interests of children at all times and to give the child's perspective appropriate weight based on his or her growing capacities. A parent's stated opposition to abortion should not automatically imply that carrying a pregnancy to term is in the best interests of the child, especially when the pregnant girl expresses a desire to terminate the pregnancy. According to a U.S. Supreme Judicial judgment, parental consent laws must provide a court procedure for waiving parental authorization in specific circumstances. Governments must ensure that this precedent is reflected in legislation that effectively protects the interests of all children.

Doctors and family members are being prosecuted.

Abortion-seeking women and girls are no longer vulnerable to criminal prosecution in the United States. However, in certain locations, family members, physicians, nurses, and friends who assist women and girls in urgent need of an abortion may be

In July 2006, the United States Senate passed a version of the Child Custody Protection Act, which had been passed in the House of Representatives as the Child Interstate Abortion Notification Act in April 2005. If this measure becomes law, any adult who aids a minor in crossing a state line to have an abortion in violation of parental consent or notification regulations in the child's home state will be charged with a federal crime.

Furthermore, numerous states have adopted legislation to penalize doctors who perform abortions on certain types of patients. The most notable exception is South Dakota's blanket abortion ban, which was signed into law in March 2006 and makes abortion illegal unless the surgery is performed to save the pregnant woman's life. Nongovernmental advocacy organizations that closely monitor abortion law changes report that a number of additional states, including Georgia, Indiana, Ohio,

Louisiana, and Tennessee, have moved to enact similar legislation.

Conclusion

Abortion is an extremely delicate subject that inspires strong feelings. On the other hand, fair access to safe and legal abortion services is first and foremost a human right. The legality of abortion coexists in the United States with onerous regulations, thinly veiled political opposition to a woman's right to make independent decisions about pregnancy and abortion, and a lack of federal and state funding for the provision of abortion services to low-income women, which severely limits women's ability to exercise this right. Women's and girls' human rights in the United States will not be fully protected unless access to safe abortion is provided.

in a brand-new medical and scientific day You live beside some extremely deadly microorganisms that are always evolving, no matter where you are. They are human adversaries. They are spread through dangerous sexual relationships and are capable of killing everyone. Even if you live in a developed country, rape is a serious medical emergency. If you are raped, it is both your job and society's responsibility to ensure your medical treatment. Forget about the police and other man-dominated patriarchal entities, as well as their masculine suggestions. Don't go to court if you don't want to. If you have been raped, get medical treatment. If you change your mind once you have cleared your mind, you might choose to aid police in putting the rapist in prison. Be aware that this is not a pleasant operation, but many jurisdictions will support you brilliantly.

We believe that governments should not legislate women's bodies. To be honest, there are so many thousands of situations in which triage practitioners must make life-or-death decisions that legislating any one medical or surgical procedure is simply insane. Doctors and their support staff are pledged to save as many lives as they can. That's all there is to it.

It may be horrifying that patriarchs want to restrict abortion. This should not happen in developed countries. Let physicians do their job. On the other hand, in destitute nations where sheer mayhem prevails, abuse of the abortion process happens too often, and when it becomes a widespread crime, it is a problem of the state.

Dealing with the abuse might be better than criminalizing abortion, but in certain countries, abuse has no bounds.

Children cannot become pregnant, yet they are all too frequently raped. Often, the crime and pregnancy are discovered too late for any other alternative except medically induced abortion or, in the worst-case scenario, surgical abortion.

Nobody should be forced to get pregnant. There are various reasons why this should not happen. If you have been raped, apply the "Plan B" medical cure as soon as possible. Don't hazard a guess. If you have been raped, you must seek medical attention for a variety of reasons. Our experience shows that in developed countries, there is no excuse for individuals not to receive medical care in these situations. You have duties as a woman in society.

Some microorganisms transmitted during intercourse are lethal if left untreated. If you are in a developed country, dial an emergency number and request an ambulance or go into a medical institution. Grow a backbone and report the rape to reliable medical personnel. You will most likely save your own life. Rape is a threat to your life. It may be, and most likely is, a serious medical emergency. Don't listen to random dudes who say it's not a big issue.

Our battle with microorganisms begins with intercourse. It's a new day on this subject. First responders' routines include pregnancy prevention and the mitigation of morbid illnesses that you could otherwise transmit. Legislators are correct to be concerned that making induced abortion available to medical practitioners encourages abortion on demand. However, most good doctors will not kill a child, so patients in developed countries are expected to get help quickly and avoid the implantation of an egg fertilized during rape. The optimum time to intervene is the morning following the rape or unprotected intercourse.

Triage is a separate story. Abortion is a medical therapy that can save lives, but it must be assessed on a case-by-case basis by the patient and doctor. When victims of a bus or plane tragedy arrive at an urgent care (emergency) center, they are not usually lucid. Life-changing decisions will be made. The first priority of medical personnel is to preserve your life. If you were pregnant and in an airplane crash, the terrible truth is that people died. We certainly hope it is not your child, but the doctors there will need to decide which lives they can save and then go about saving those lives. Legislators who interfere with the process are completely in the dark and will remain so until they obtain their medical degrees, licenses, and a personal inventory of practice experience. In other words, butt out.

You should never consider abortion as a method of birth control because, for one thing, murdering your child is a crime, and professionals are called to save lives, not take them. Keep it in mind. Read on to find out when your egg has developed into a child. If something is going to happen, it will happen soon.

The doctor must make a dreadful decision during an induced abortion.

Most governments are led by males. For millennia, the males of these patriarchs have spent a significant amount of time controlling what women may and cannot do with their bodies.

This has to stop.

For example, legislating induced abortion is a fool's errand. You can rely on the medical profession to perform its job. Interfering with it results in far too many deaths.

Abortion as a method of birth control is unethical. That would be the equivalent of murdering a kid. You have influence over your body and what it does. But after you've used your body to create a new life, don't dare remove it. Consider the consequences of a murder conviction before taking a child's life. If you need an induced abortion for genuine medical reasons, you will have it regardless of the legislation, just because your doctor has pledged to save the lives he or she can. Meanwhile, at a time when contraception is so simple and widely available, using abortion as a method of birth control is tantamount to murder. Today is a new day. Throw off what you thought you knew and start again, learning.

If you don't want to have a child, use contraception or avoid intercourse. Once a human being is created, the Universal Declaration of Human Rights takes effect, and the right to life takes precedence.

Canada decriminalized abortion more than 30 years ago when its highest court struck down a section of the Criminal Code that criminalized abortion.

Regardless of the Jan. 28, 1988 decision, the vast majority of Canadian hospitals do not offer abortions on demand, and some provinces lack dedicated abortion facilities.

Medical rules, codes of ethics, and procedures control the induced abortion process in Canada.

Most conscientious professionals respect the rights of the unborn child. Those who do not should face criminal charges.

Yes, some of the violations of the 1988 judgment are not being investigated and should be. Individuals, for example, travel to Canada to conduct "female infanticide"—killing the unwanted child because of its gender. The Morgentaler Clinics, a quasi-abortion retail network founded by Doctor Henry Morgentaler, who discovered the breach in the Canadian Criminal Code and convinced the Supreme Court to overturn the statute, have slaughtered countless newborns as a kind of on-demand birth control.

As a result, Canada, one of only a few countries that (possibly unintentionally) decriminalized the medical practice of induced abortion, suffers little abuse. However, these violations are grave and should be punished.

Doctors who perform induced abortions on demand as a method of birth control are committing the crime of child murder and should be punished as such.

Doctors who are forced to choose between the life of the patient mother and the life of the patient fetus must save the life or lives that can be saved without intervention.

Many doctors are realistically pessimistic about the strength and application of medical rules, codes of ethics, and procedures, and they advocate for the criminalization of induced abortion on demand. The RINJ Foundation medical teams often believe that governments such as Canada must do more to avoid abuses of their current lack of anti-abortion legislation before the international medical community is completely convinced that decriminalizing abortion is appropriate. What Canada is on its way to proving is that decriminalizing induced abortion is possible while still protecting the sanctity of life, if not now, then in the future. The next best approach is to prosecute the murder of unborn infants, which is basic law enforcement. Any government omission or action that jeopardizes the sanctity of life is unquestionably damaging.

The goal is to combat abuses, not medical practices themselves.

We must listen to our medical brothers and sisters and allow them to carry out their duties in accordance with their best medical practices and code of ethics.

There is much too much impunity in the world for all types of murders. Overpopulation is causing hiccups in human development as well as immoral ideas about the value of human life. Can we recover the sanctity of life while keeping a reasonable population and total fertility rate in place?

You can help by:

Write letters to your federal and state senators and representatives urging them to provide equal access to reproductive health care, including modern contraception, emergency contraception, and voluntary abortion services. Several measures have already been offered to address these issues. You should specifically ask your federal congressperson to support

S.1264/H.R.2928 is the Compassionate Assistance for Rape Emergencies Act. This bill would require survivors of sexual assault to be given the "morning-after" pill at the emergency room.

S.2593/H.R.5151 is the Freedom of Choice Act. FOCA guarantees a woman's right to choose whether or not to have a child or to terminate a pregnancy without interference from the state or others.

Note

<u>*Note*</u>

9 798839 834415